BARN STAR ✶ SAMPLER

20 STARRY BLOCKS AND 7 SPECTACULAR QUILTS

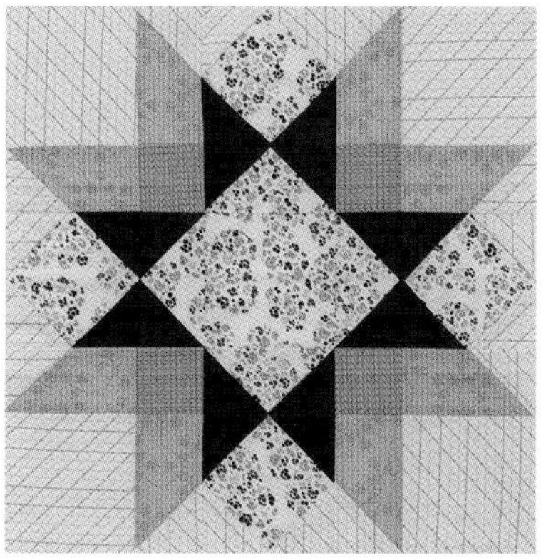

SHELLEY CAVANNA

T0308639

C&T PUBLISHING
Another Maker Inspired!

Copyright © 2022 by Michelle N. Cavanna

Publisher: Amy Barrett-Daffin

Creative Director: Gailen Runge

Senior Editor: Roxane Cerda

Technical Editor: Nancy Mahoney

Cover And Interior Designer: Adrienne Smitke

Copy Editor: Taylor ffitch

Illustrator: Sandy Loi

Photographer: Brent Kane

Production Coordinator: Zinnia Heinzmann

Published by C&T Publishing, Inc., P.O. Box 1456, Lafayette, CA 94549

All rights reserved. No part of this work covered by the copyright hereon may be used in any form or reproduced by any means—graphic, electronic, or mechanical, including photocopying, recording, taping, or information storage and retrieval systems—without written permission from the publisher. The copyrights on individual artworks are retained by the artists as noted in *Barn Star Sampler*. These designs may be used to make items for personal use only and may not be used for the purpose of personal profit. Items created to benefit nonprofit groups, or that will be publicly displayed, must be conspicuously labeled with the following credit: "Designs copyright © 2022 by Shelley Cavanna from the book *Barn Star Sampler* from C&T Publishing, Inc." Permission for all other purposes must be requested in writing from C&T Publishing, Inc.

Attention Teachers: C&T Publishing, Inc., encourages the use of our books as texts for teaching. You can find lesson plans for many of our titles at ctpub.com or contact us at ctinfo@ctpub.com.

We take great care to ensure that the information included in our products is accurate and presented in good faith, but no warranty is provided, nor are results guaranteed. Having no control over the choices of materials or procedures used, neither the author nor C&T Publishing, Inc., shall have any liability to any person or entity with respect to any loss or damage caused directly or indirectly by the information contained in this book. For your convenience, we post an up-to-date listing of corrections on our website (ctpub.com). If a correction is not already noted, please contact our customer service department at ctinfo@ctpub.com or P.O. Box 1456, Lafayette, CA 94549.

Trademark (™) and registered trademark (®) names are used throughout this book. Rather than use the symbols with every occurrence of a trademark or registered trademark name, we are using the names only in the editorial fashion and to the benefit of the owner, with no intention of infringement.

Library of Congress Control Number: 2023931942

Printed in the USA

10 9 8 7 6 5

SPECIAL THANKS

Photography for this book was taken at the Garden Barn in Indianola, Iowa, and the home of Samantha Keltner in Des Moines, Iowa.

DEDICATION

For Mom, my quilting partner in crime.
And for Dad, for building us the studio of our dreams!

CONTENTS

INTRODUCTION

Have you ever been driving through the country and stumbled upon a painted quilt block hanging, like a piece of art, on the side of a barn?

Surprisingly, the idea of a "barn quilt" is a relatively recent idea. Early German and Swiss settlers in southeastern Pennsylvania (known as Pennsylvania Dutch) painted hex signs on their barns to share their folk-art heritage and to bring good fortune. But it was 200 years later when the first known barn quilt was installed in Adams County, Ohio, in the early 2000s by Donna Sue Groves, in honor of her quilting mother. After quickly realizing how popular the barn quilt was, the local community started a grassroots movement to decorate other local barns and buildings with painted quilts. The hope was to create a "quilt trail map" that would attract tourists.

The idea spread like wildfire. . . and twenty years later you can find quilt trails in almost every state in the US! Barn quilts are sometimes modeled after a block used in a family heirloom quilt or based on a classic design that shares something about the barn owners—a Nine Patch to represent nine grandchildren, or a Carpenter Star for a woodworking grandfather. The barn quilts became a way to celebrate family and cultural heritage, to tell stories the of the community, and to lead visitors around to places of historical importance that they might have missed otherwise.

My family lives in the heart of Gold Country in Northern California. With Sacramento marking the end of the California trail, we're surround by a rich history of the gold rush and pioneer tradition. So, it isn't surprising that five of the six California counties with official barn quilt trails are right here in the Gold Country region. In these counties, communities have come together to display artfully painted quilt blocks on barns and historical buildings, right along the many overland trails followed by the pioneers and the gold rush '49ers. These trails let us walk in their footsteps and find treasures in the form of quilt blocks all along the way.

As a family, we love the outdoors and exploring our state, and it's always the icing on the cake when we spot a barn quilt tucked along a scenic country road. The Barn Star Sampler quilt, the star of this book, was inspired by these adventures on the roads-less-traveled, and is a celebration of finding art and beauty in unexpected places.

Happy sewing!

~Shelley

HOW TO USE THIS BOOK

This book is a celebration of some of my very favorite starry quilt blocks! The star of this show is a sampler quilt, which uses 20 different block designs (ranging in size from 4" to 24") in a fresh and modern sampler-quilt layout.

In addition to the sampler quilt, you'll find six more projects that showcase just a few blocks in more traditional quilt layouts. From lap quilts to wall hangings, and even a table runner designed to use up leftover triangle trimmings, there are plenty of star-studded patterns to set your world aglow.

We had to think creatively about how to fit the patterns for seven quilt designs, along with 20 different blocks. So take a minute or two to read through this section, as it explains where to find materials lists, cutting lists for blocks and projects, and how to follow along with the cutting icons to make sure you cut exactly the right pieces for the design you're making.

The Fabrics

I used a total of 28 different prints in my Barn Star Sampler (page 11), but some of the prints used are similar in color. To make it easy for you see which print is used where, have a look at the fabric swatch list on pages 11 and 12 to see not only the color names and numbers, but also what each print looks like. These 28 fabrics are all used in the sampler; the same fabrics are used in the remaining projects, although those projects may use just six or seven of the prints, not all 28.

> **Stay on Track**
>
> **If you're switching up the colors and doing your own thing—great! But you'll definitely want to keep track of your own swatches so you know which print is fabric 1 and which is fabric 23. For a free printable swatch sheet where you can attach snippets of your fabrics, visit www.CorasQuilts.com/barn-stars.**

The Material Lists

Each quilt has its own materials list so you'll know how much of each fabric you need to make the pictured quilt. Whether you're making the Barn Star Sampler or the Baking Day table runner (page 71), when you turn to that project in the book, you'll find a list of fabrics used along with the yardage requirements for that particular quilt.

The Cutting Lists

Each quilt also has its own cutting list, with all the cutting information needed for the sashing, borders and binding. The cutting instructions for the individual blocks, however, are only listed in the blocks section of this book, starting with Block 1 on page 13. Please note: The block cutting lists will only yield the pieces needed to make one block.

Each of the seven projects specify which block(s) were used and how many of each you'll need. So, to cut the materials for your blocks, turn to the block section, find the block(s) you're making, and follow the cutting instructions, repeating as many times as needed to yield the number of blocks for your particular project.

The Cutting Icons

To make the cutting lists short and sweet, we've used icons to indicate which type of shape you need to cut. Be sure to pay close attention while cutting, because some squares might need to be cut diagonally in half or in quarters, The four icons we'll be using are:

- □ Square
- ▭ Piece or strip
- ⧄ Square cut in half diagonally to yield 2 triangles
- ⊠ Square cut into quarters diagonally to yield 4 triangles

To simplify things even more, each piece in the cutting instructions is also labeled with a letter in parentheses. The assembly diagrams refer to each piece by these letters, making it easy to see exactly where each piece is used in your block. See the example below.

From the raspberry floral, cut:
12 □ 2½" × 2½" (A)

From the light gold floral, cut:
4 ▭ 2½" × 4½" (B)
4 □ 2½" × 2½" (D)

From the gold floral, cut:
1 □ 4½" × 4½" (C)

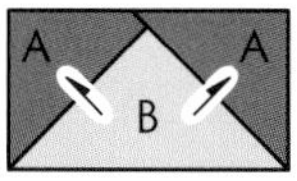

Make 12 units,
2½" × 4½".

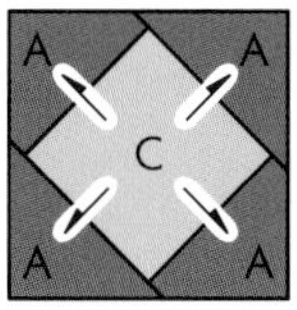

Make 3 units,
4½" × 4½".

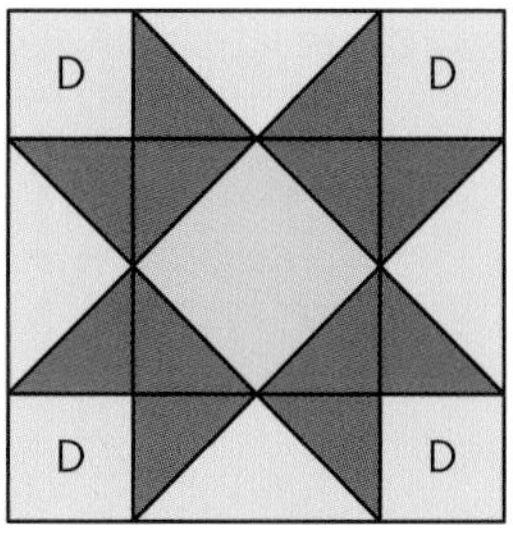

Make 3 blocks,
8½" × 8½".

Have Fun!

I know this seems like a lot of information, but trust me—everything will come together beautifully as you start piecing your first blocks. And I think you'll love having those icons and letters to tell you at a glance exactly what to do with the pieces. So, pick a project, choose your fabric, and let's make some Star blocks!

THE BARN STAR SAMPLER

With our starry sampler quilt, the journey through all those gorgeous blocks—and the discoveries made along the way—will be just as beautiful as the finished quilt!

FINISHED QUILT: 80½" × 100½"

Materials for Blocks

Yardage is based on 42"-wide fabric. Fat quarters are 18" × 21". Fat eighths are 9" × 21". The materials list that follows includes all the yardage needed to make the Barn Star Sampler quilt (or put together a full quilt kit). Fabric requirements for each set of blocks are listed on the individual block pages if you'd rather sew the sampler as a block-of-the-month project.

Fabric 1: 5/8 yard of white-and-raspberry print

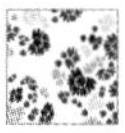
Fabric 2: 3/4 yard of white-and-raspberry floral

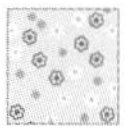
Fabric 3: 3/8 yard of coral floral

Fabric 4: 1/2 yard of coral print

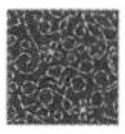
Fabric 5: 1 1/4 yards of raspberry floral

Fabric 6: 3/8 yard of raspberry print

Fabric 7: 3/8 yard of dark raspberry floral

Fabric 8: 1/4 yard of dark raspberry print

Fabric 9: 3/4 yard of plum floral

Fabric 10: 1 1/8 yards of light gold floral

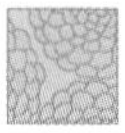
Fabric 11: 3/4 yard of gold floral

Fabric 12: 1/2 yard of green print #1

Fabric 13: 7/8 yard of green print #2

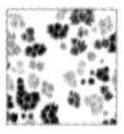
Fabric 14: 1 1/4 yards of aqua floral #1

Fabric 15: 3/8 yard of aqua floral #2

Fabric 16: 3/4 yard of light aqua print

Continued on page 12

Continued from page 11

Fabric 17: ½ yard of aqua print

Fabric 18: ⅜ yard of medium aqua print

Fabric 19: ½ yard of teal print

Fabric 20: ¾ yard of teal floral

Fabric 21: 1 yard of indigo floral

Fabric 22: 1 yard of indigo print

Fabric 23: ¾ yard of dark indigo print

Fabric 24: 1 yard of white solid

Fabric 25: 2¼ yards of white print #1

Fabric 26: 1⅝ yards of white print #2

Fabric 27: 2 yards of light gray print #1

Fabric 28: ⅜ yard of light gray print #2

Cutting

All measurements include ¼"-wide seam allowances. I recommend that you always look through your scraps and cut pieces from any remaining strips left over from other blocks before cutting new strips. Label your pieces as you cut. The assembly diagrams refer to each piece by the letter that follows the dimensions. Materials and cutting instructions are separated by block. For each block, the materials listed yield the number of blocks needed to make the Barn Star Sampler. If you are making a different quilt, refer to the materials list for that project. For each block, the cutting instructions yield the pieces needed to make one block. Check the instructions for the project you're making to see how many blocks to cut. Assembly is for one block at a time; refer to page 39 to see how many of each block is needed for the Barn Star Sampler. Measurements listed for assembled pieces include seam allowances.

BLOCK 1

DIAMOND STAR

FINISHED BLOCK: 24" × 24"

Materials

Materials are for making 2 identical blocks needed for the Barn Star Sampler. If you are making a different quilt, refer to the materials list for that project.

1¼ yards of white print #1 for background (fabric 25)

⅜ yard of dark indigo print for corner and center units (fabric 23)

1 fat quarter of green print #1 for corner and side units (fabric 12)

1 fat quarter of aqua floral #2 for side units (fabric 15)

⅜ yard of indigo floral for side units (fabric 21)

1 fat eighth of medium aqua print for center units (fabric 18)

Cutting for 1 Block

The instructions yield pieces needed to make 1 block. Check the instructions for the project you're making to see how many blocks are needed. Label your pieces as you cut. The assembly diagrams refer to each piece by the letter that follows the dimensions.

From white print #1, cut:
16 □ 3" × 3" (A)
16 □ 2½" × 2½" (C)
4 □ 4½" × 4½" (E)
16 ▭ 2½" × 4½" (G)
8 ▭ 2½" × 6½" (H)
1 ⊠ 5½" × 5½" (L)

From the dark indigo print, cut:
16 □ 3" × 3" (B)
1 □ 4½" × 4½" (K)

From green print #1, cut:
8 □ 2½" × 2½" (D)
8 ▭ 2½" × 4½" (F)

From aqua floral #2, cut:
8 ▭ 2½" × 4½" (I)

From the indigo floral, cut:
8 □ 4½" × 4½" (J)

From the medium aqua print, cut:
2 ⧄ 5" × 5" (M)

Making the Corner Units

Instructions are for making one block. Press seam allowances as indicated by the arrows.

1. Use the A and B squares to make 32 half-square-triangle units (see page 77) and trim them to 2½" square.

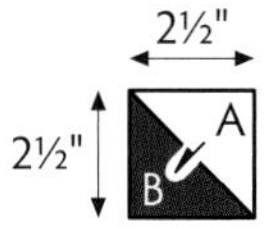

Make 32 units.

2. Join a triangle unit and a C square. Make four units measuring 2½" × 4½".

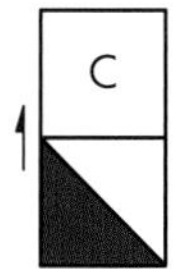

Make 4 units, 2½" × 4½".

3. Sew C and D squares to opposite sides of a triangle unit. Make four units measuring 2½" × 6½".

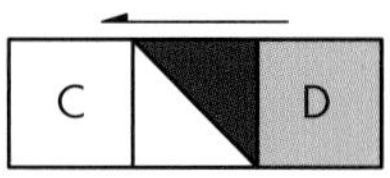

Make 4 units, 2½" × 6½".

4. Join three triangle units as shown. Make four units measuring 2½" × 6½".

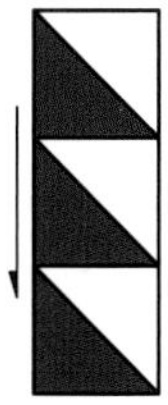
Make 4 units, 2½" × 6½".

5. Join three triangle units and a D square. Make four units measuring 2½" × 8½".

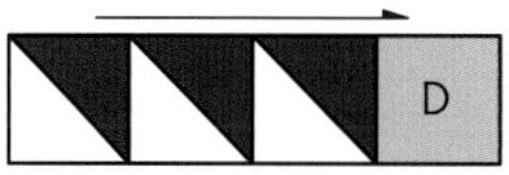

Make 4 units, 2½" × 8½".

6. Pressing after each seam, join one unit each from steps 2–5 and one E square as shown. Make four corner units measuring 8½" square.

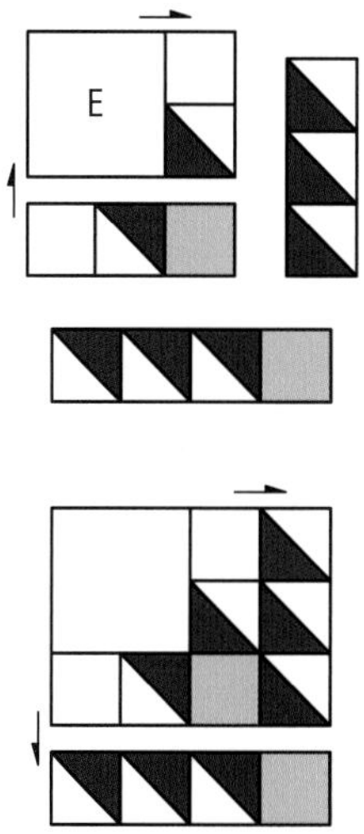

Make 4 units, 8½" × 8½".

Making the Side Units

1. Use F and G pieces to make eight elongated flying-geese units (see page 76) measuring 2½" × 8½".

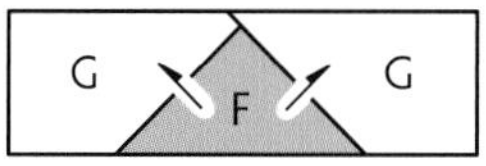

Make 8 units, 2½" × 8½".

2. Sew an H piece to the right end of an I piece as shown. Sew a C square to the left end of the I piece. Make four units measuring 2½" × 8½".

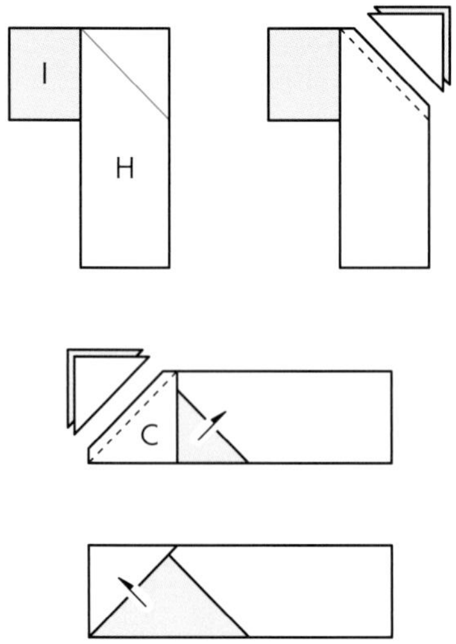

Make 4 units,
2½" × 8½".

> ### KEEP IT TOGETHER
>
> **If you plan to press seam allowances open, it's a good idea to backstitch at the beginning and end of a seam. Backstitching will add a bit of stability and ensure that your seams don't unravel as you're assembling the blocks.**

3. Sew an H piece to the left end of an I piece and then sew a C square to the right end of the I piece. Make four units measuring 2½" × 8½". Note that the units should be mirror images of the units from step 2.

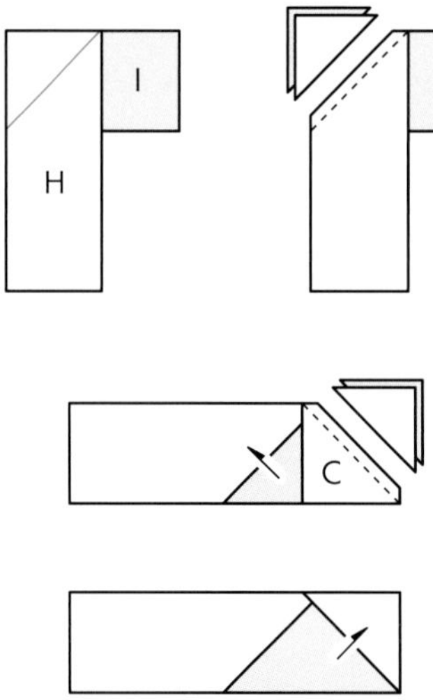

Make 4 units,
2½" × 8½".

4. Join two units from step 1 and one unit each from steps 2 and 3. Make four units measuring 8½" square.

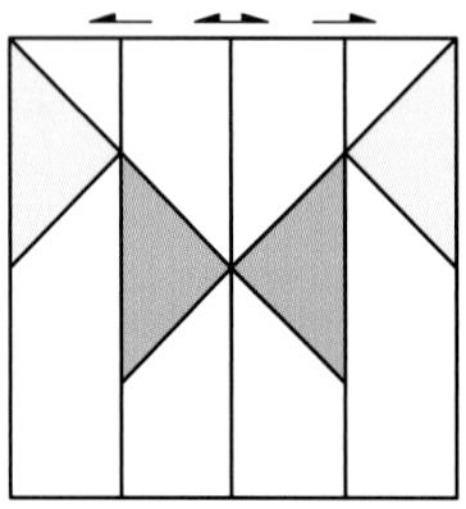

Make 4 units,
8½" × 8½".

5. Sew a J square to the lower-left corner of a unit from step 4. Sew a J square to the lower-right corner. Make four side units measuring 8½" square.

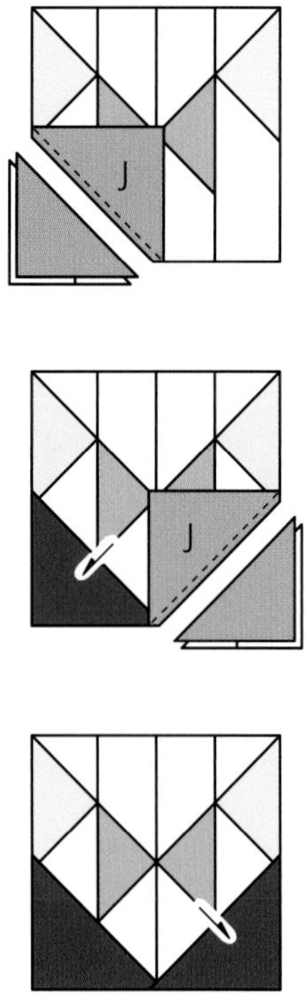

Make 4 units,
8½" × 8½".

Making the Center Unit

1. Sew two L triangles to opposite sides of the K square and press. Repeat to add L triangles to the remaining sides. Trim the unit to 6⅛" square, making sure to leave ¼" beyond all the points of the K square for seam allowances.

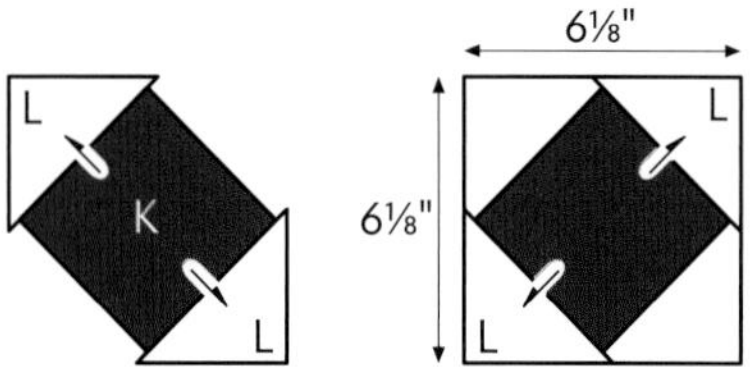

Make 1 unit.

2. Sew two M triangles to opposite sides of the unit from step 1 and press. Repeat to add M triangles to the remaining sides. Trim the unit to 8½" square, making sure to leave ¼" beyond all the points of the L square for seam allowances.

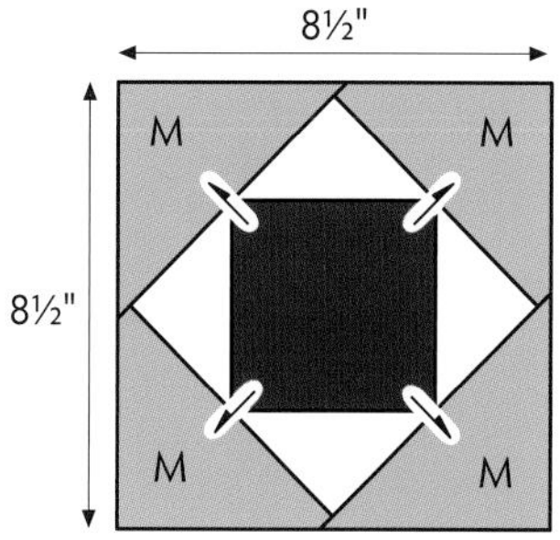

Make 1 unit.

Assembling Block 1

Arrange four corner units, four side units, and one center unit in three rows. Sew the units into rows and then join the rows. Make one block measuring 24½" square.

Make 1 block, 24½" × 24½".

BLOCK 2

CHRISTMAS STAR

FINISHED BLOCK: 24" × 24"

Materials

Materials are for making 2 identical blocks needed for the Barn Star Sampler.

 ⅞ yard of white print #2 for background (fabric 26)

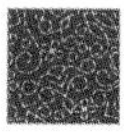 ⅜ yard of raspberry floral for corner units (fabric 5)

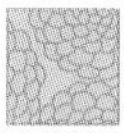 ⅜ yard of gold floral for corner units (fabric 11)

 1 fat quarter of raspberry print for side units and center square (fabric 6)

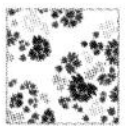 ½ yard of white-and-raspberry floral for side units (fabric 2)

 ½ yard of light gold floral for side units (fabric 10)

Cutting for 1 Block

The instructions yield pieces needed to make 1 block. Check the instructions for the project you're making to see how many blocks are needed. Label your pieces as you cut. The assembly diagrams refer to each piece by the letter that follows the dimensions.

From white print #2, cut:
2 □ 4" × 4" (A)
12 ▭ 3½" × 6½" (F)
8 □ 3½" × 3½" (C)

From the raspberry floral, cut:
2 □ 4" × 4" (B)
4 ▭ 3½" × 6½" (D)

From the gold floral, cut:
4 □ 3½" × 3½" (E)
4 ▭ 3½" × 6½" (G)

From the raspberry print, cut:
8 □ 3½" × 3½" (H)
1 □ 6½" × 6½" (M)

From the white-and-raspberry floral, cut:
4 ▭ 3½" × 6½" (I)
8 □ 3½" × 3½" (J)

From the light gold floral, cut:
4 ▭ 3½" × 6½" (K)
8 □ 3½" × 3½" (L)

Making the Corner Units

Instructions are for making one block. Press seam allowances as indicated by the arrows.

1. Use A and B squares to make four half-square-triangle units (see page 77) and trim them to 3½" square.

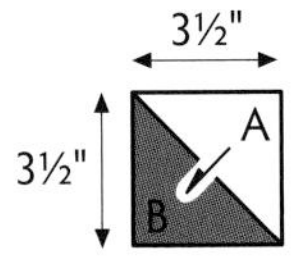

Make 4 units.

2. Sew a C square to the left end of a D piece (see page 74). Make four units measuring 3½" × 6½".

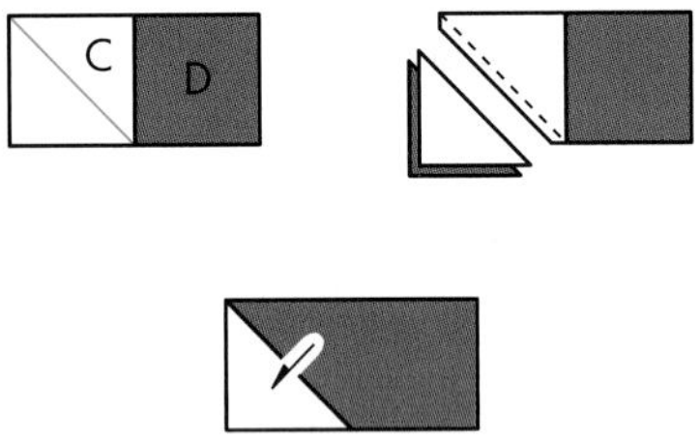

Make 4 units,
3½" × 6½".

3. Sew an E square to the left end of an F piece. Make four units measuring 3½" × 6½".

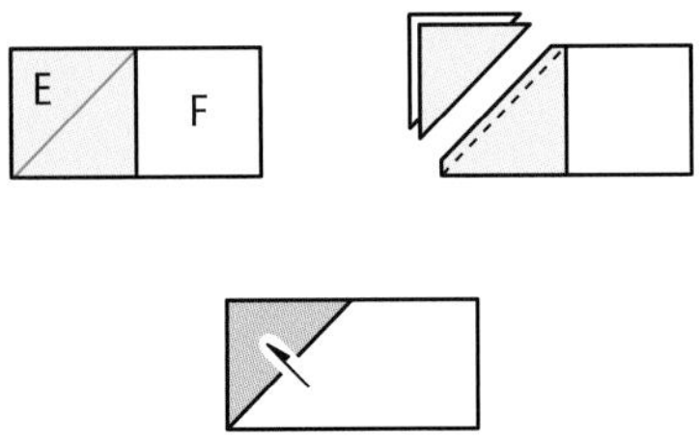

Make 4 units,
3½" × 6½".

4. Sew a G piece to the right end of an F piece (see page 76). Make four units measuring 3½" × 9½".

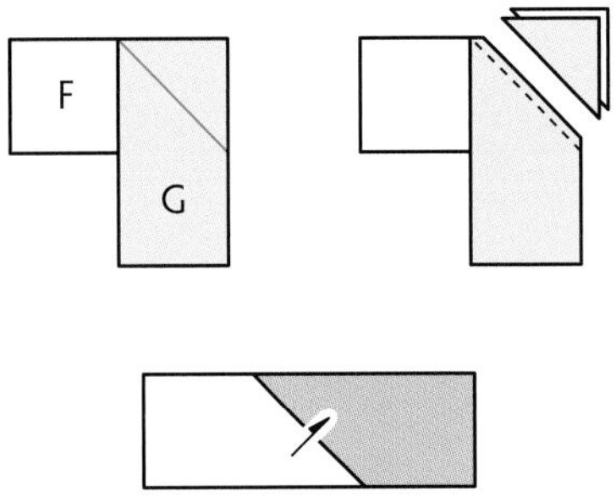

Make 4 units,
3½" × 9½".

5. Pressing after each seam, join one unit each from steps 1–4 and one C square as shown. Make four corner units measuring 9½" square.

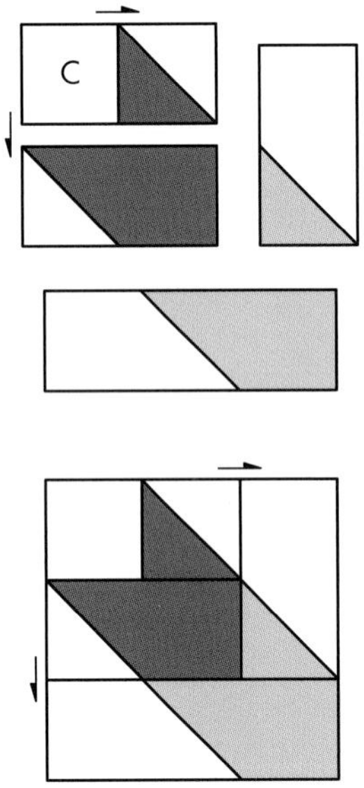

Make 4 units,
9½" × 9½".

Making the Side Units

1. Use the H, J, and L squares and the I, K, and F pieces to make four flying-geese units of each color combination (see page 75). The units should measure 3½" × 6½".

Make 4 units,
3½" × 6½".

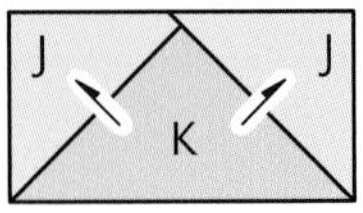

Make 4 units,
3½" × 6½".

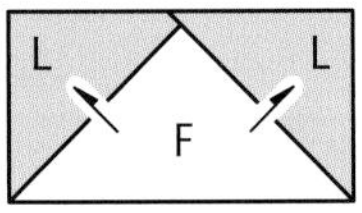

Make 4 units,
3½" × 6½".

2. Join one of each of the units from step 1 as shown. Make four side units measuring 6½" × 9½".

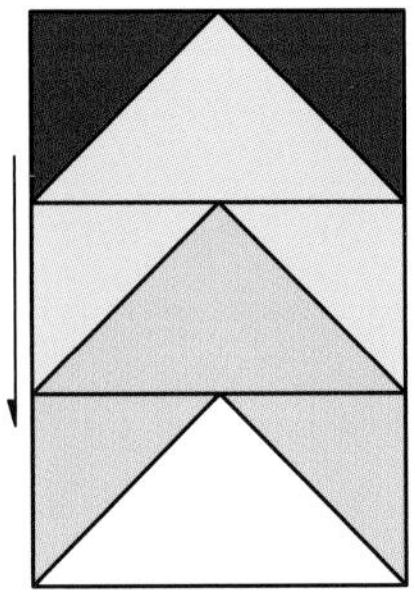

Make 4 units,
6½" × 9½".

Good Neighbors

Pressing for the side units in step 2 might seem a little backward from what you would expect, but pressing the unit in this manner will allow the seam allowances to nest together nicely.

Assembling Block 2

Arrange the four corner units, four side units, and one M square in three rows. Sew all the pieces into rows and then join the rows. Make one block measuring 24½" square.

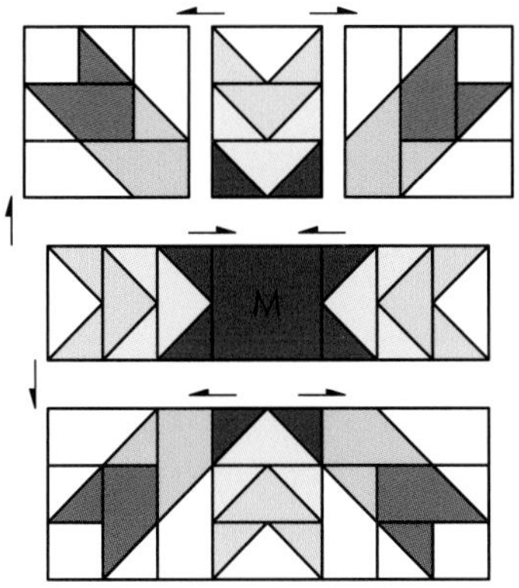

Make 1 block, 24½" × 24½".

BLOCK 3

CARPENTER STAR

FINISHED BLOCK: 24" × 24"

Materials

Materials are for making 2 identical blocks needed for the Barn Star Sampler. If you are making a different quilt, refer to the materials list for that project.

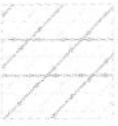 ¾ yard of light gray print #1 for background (fabric 27)

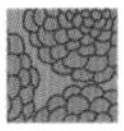 ⅜ yard of teal floral for corner units (fabric 20)

 ⅜ yard of green print #2 for corner units (fabric 13)

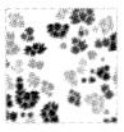 ½ yard of aqua floral #1 for corner and side units (fabric 14)

 1 fat quarter of teal print for side units (fabric 19)

 ⅜ yard of indigo print for side and center units (fabric 22)

Cutting for 1 Block

The instructions yield pieces needed to make 1 block. Check the instructions for the project you're making to see how many blocks are needed. Label your pieces as you cut. The assembly diagrams refer to each piece by the letter that follows the dimensions.

From light gray print #1, cut:
12 ☐ 3½" × 3½" (A)
4 ▭ 3½" × 6½" (C)
1 ☒ 7½" × 7½" (F)
1 ☐ 6½" × 6½" (K)

From the teal floral, cut:
12 ☐ 3½" × 3½" (B)

From green print #2, cut:
8 ▭ 3½" × 6½" (D)

From aqua floral #1, cut:
4 ☐ 3½" × 3½" (E)
4 ▭ 3½" × 6½" (J)
1 ☒ 7½" × 7½" (H)

From the teal print, cut:
2 ☒ 7½" × 7½" (G)

From the indigo print, cut:
12 ☐ 3½" × 3½" (I)

Making the Corner Units

Instructions are for making one block. Press seam allowances as indicated by the arrows.

1. Join A and B squares. Sew a C piece to the top. Make four units measuring 6½" square.

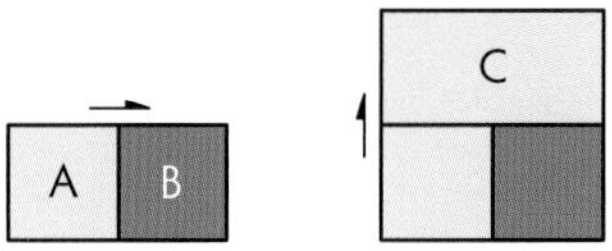

Make 4 units, 6½" × 6½".

2. Sew A and B squares to the left and right ends of a D piece as shown (see page 74). Make four units measuring 3½" × 6½". Repeat to make four mirror-image units.

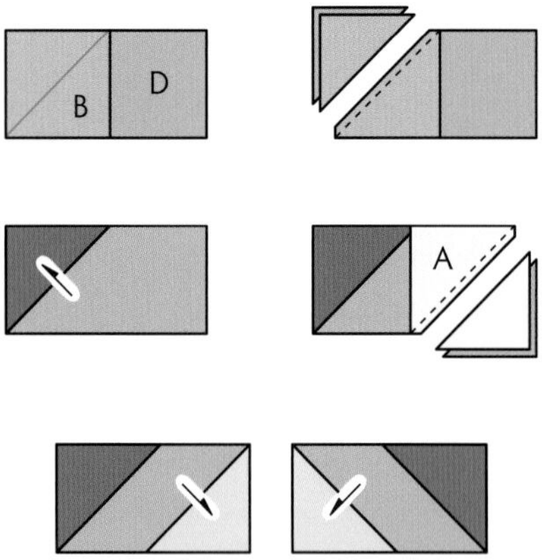

Make 4 of each unit,
3½" × 6½".

3. Arrange one E square and one of each unit from steps 1 and 2 as shown. Sew the units into rows and then join the rows. Make four units measuring 9½" square.

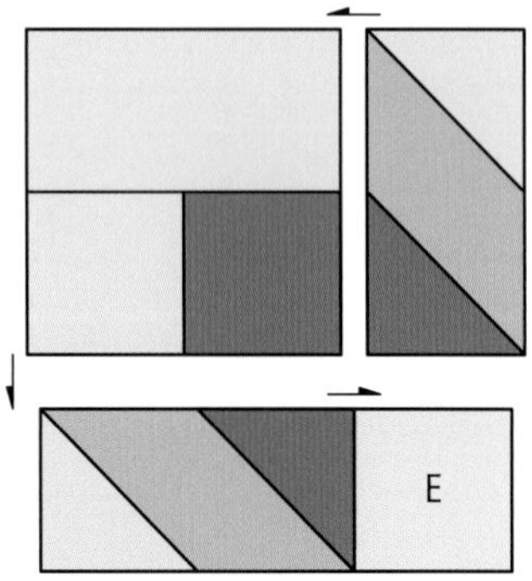

Make 4 units,
9½" × 9½".

Making the Side Units

1. Join F, G, and H triangles to make four hourglass units. Press the center seam so that it lies flat (see below). Trim the units to 6½" square (see page 77).

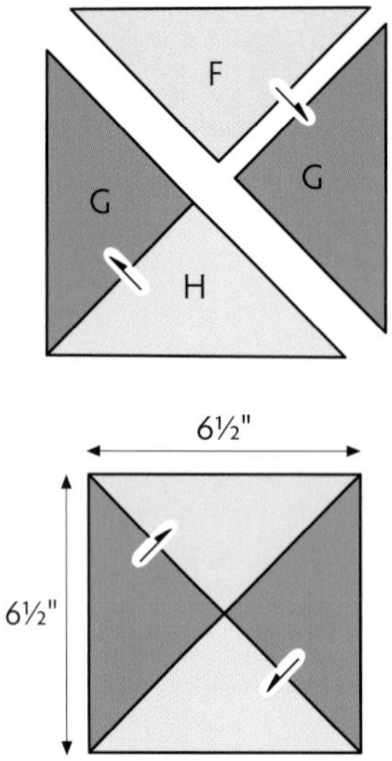

Make 4 units.

2. Use the I squares and J pieces to make four flying-geese units (see page 75) measuring 3½" × 6½".

Make 4 units,
3½" × 6½".

3. Join the units from steps 1 and 2 as shown. Make four side units measuring 6½" × 9½".

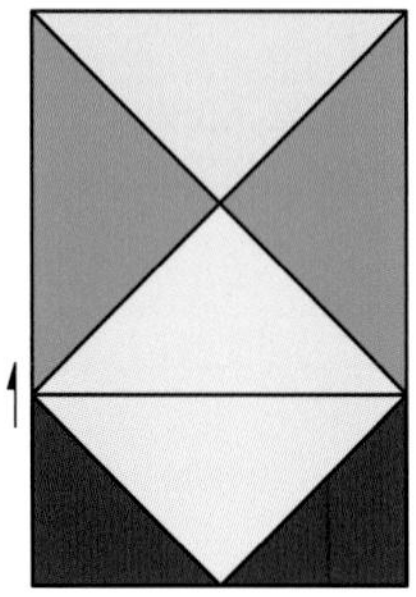

Make 4 units,
6½" × 9½".

Pressing Matters

Pressing seam allowances in a clockwise or counterclockwise direction will help reduce bulk. To press in this manner, use a seam ripper to remove the stitching above the horizontal seam allowance. From the back of the unit, finger-press the seam allowances in the desired direction. Turn the unit over and press from the front with an iron.

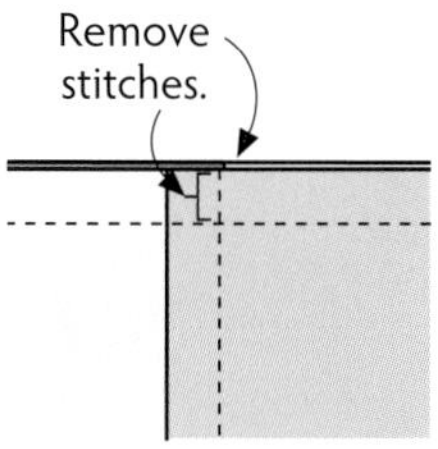

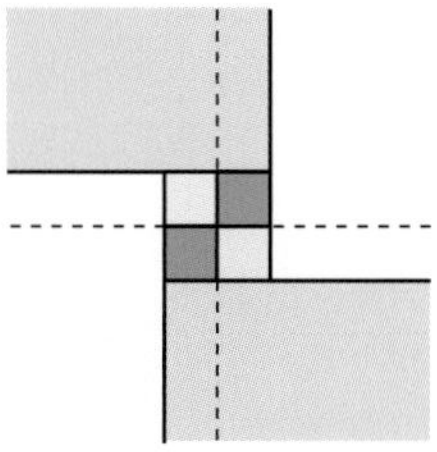

Making the Center Units

Use I and K squares to make one square-in-a-square unit (see page 76) measuring 6½" square.

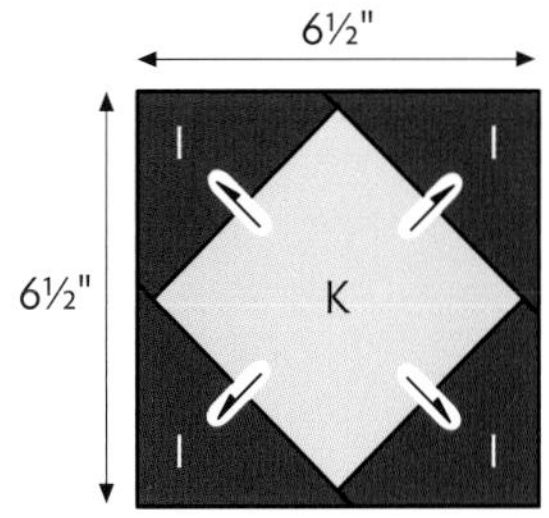

Make 1 unit.

Assembling Block 3

Arrange four corner units, four side units, and one center unit in three rows. Sew the units into rows and then join the rows. Make one block measuring 24½" square.

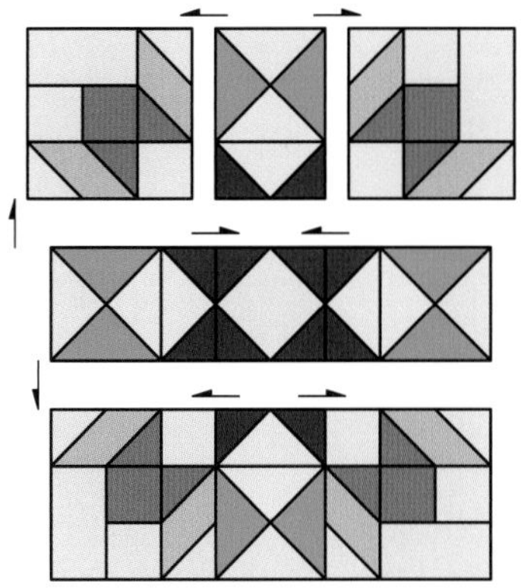

Make 1 block, 24½" × 24½".

BLOCK 4

TULIP STAR

FINISHED BLOCK: 16" × 16"

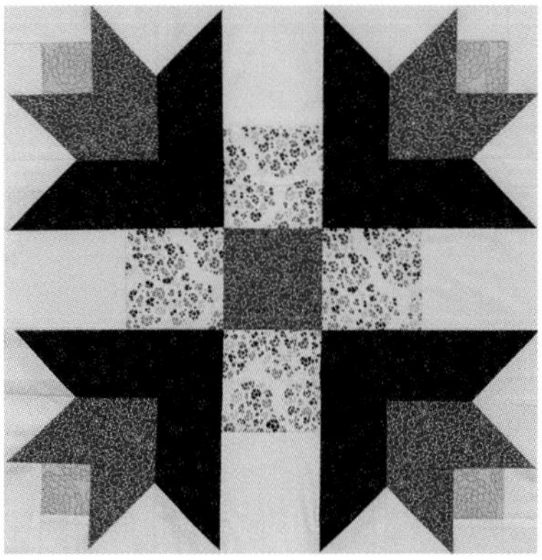

Materials

Materials are for making 2 identical blocks needed for the Barn Star Sampler.

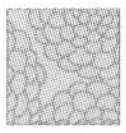 1 square, 10" × 10", of gold floral for corner units (fabric 11)

 ⅜ yard of white solid for background (fabric 24)

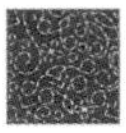 1 fat quarter of raspberry floral for corner units and center square (fabric 5)

 1 fat quarter of plum floral for corner units (fabric 9)

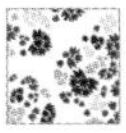 1 fat eighth of white-and-raspberry floral for side units (fabric 2)

Cutting for 1 Block

The instructions yield pieces needed to make 1 block. Check the instructions for the project you're making to see how many blocks are needed. Label your pieces as you cut. The assembly diagrams refer to each piece by the letter that follows the dimensions.

From the gold floral, cut:
4 □ 2" × 2" (A)

From the white solid, cut:
4 ▭ 1½" × 2" (B)
4 ▭ 1½" × 3" (C)
16 □ 2½" × 2½" (F)
4 ▭ 3½" × 4" (I)

From the raspberry floral, cut:
4 ▭ 2½" × 3" (D)
4 ▭ 2½" × 5" (E)
1 □ 3½" × 3½" (K)

From the plum floral, cut:
4 ▭ 2½" × 5" (G)
4 ▭ 2½" × 7" (H)

From the white-and-raspberry floral, cut:
4 □ 3½" × 3½" (J)

Making the Corner Units

Instructions are for making one block. Press seam allowances as indicated by the arrows.

1. Join an A square and a B piece. Sew a C piece to the top. Make four units measuring 3" square.

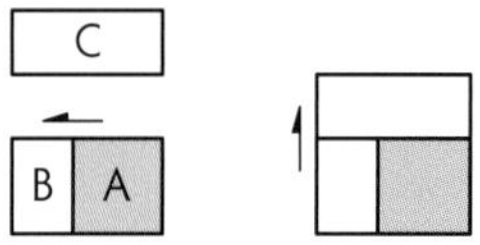

Make 4 units, 3" × 3".

2. Sew a D piece to the right edge of a unit from step 1. Sew an E piece to the bottom edge. Make four units measuring 5" square.

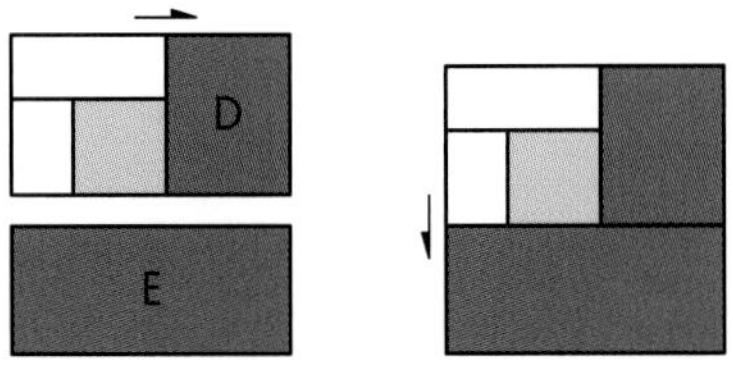

Make 4 units,
5" × 5".

3. Sew F squares to the upper-right and lower-left corners of a unit from step 2 (see page 74). Make four units measuring 5" square.

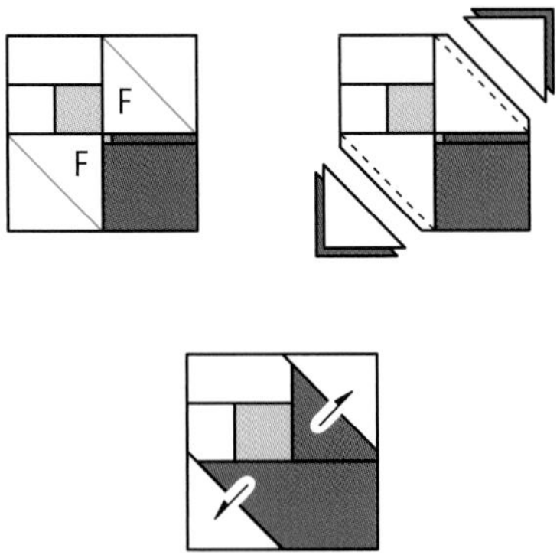

Make 4 units,
5" × 5".

4. Sew an F square to the right end of a G piece (see page 74). Make four units measuring 2½" × 5".

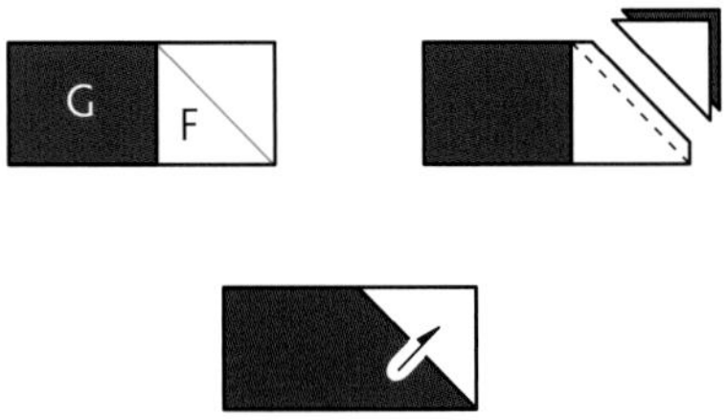

Make 4 units,
2½" × 5".

5. Sew an F square to the left end of an H piece. Make four units measuring 2½" × 7".

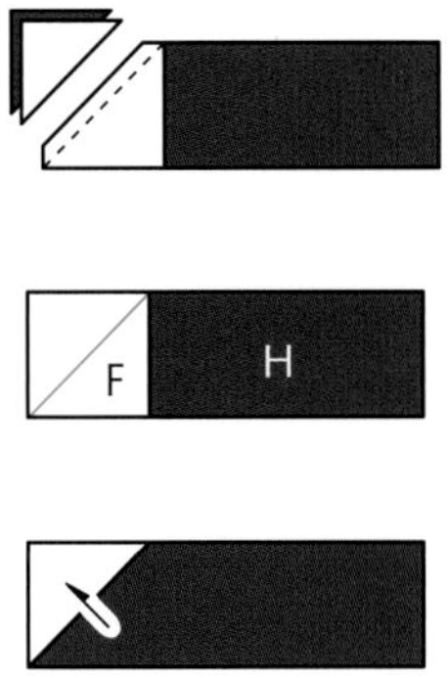

Make 4 units,
2½" × 7".

6. Sew a unit from step 4 to the right side of a unit from step 3. Sew a unit from step 5 to the bottom. Make four corner units measuring 7" square.

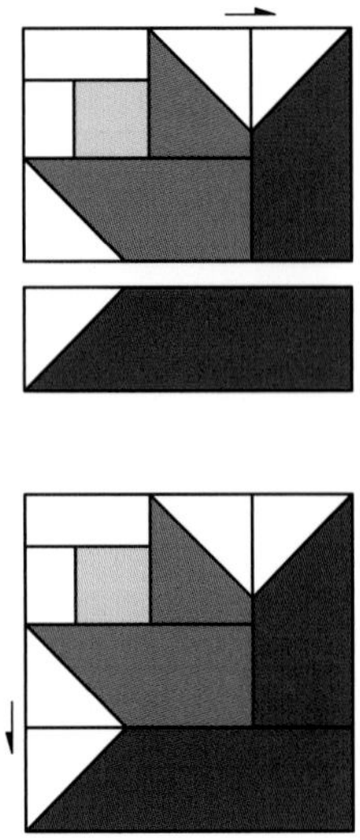

Make 4 units,
7" × 7".

Making the Side Units

Join an I piece and a J square. Make four units measuring 3½" × 7".

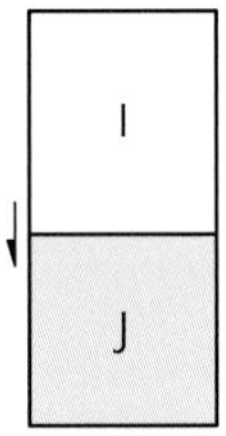

Make 4 units,
3½" × 7".

Assembling Block 4

Arrange four corner units, four side units, and one K square in three rows. Sew all the pieces into rows and then join the rows. Make one block measuring 16½" square.

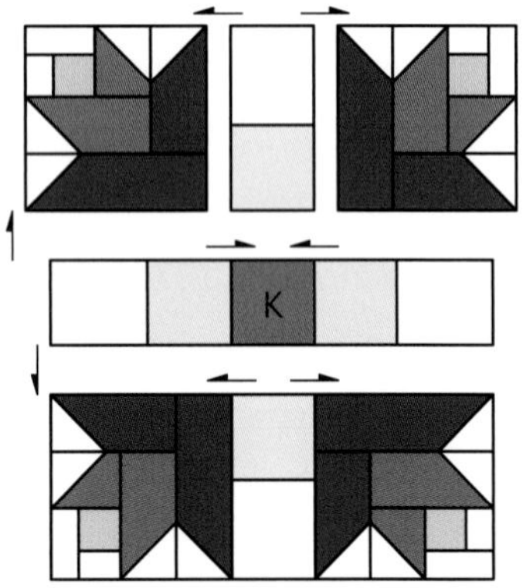

Make 1 block,
16½" × 16½".

BLOCK 5

NORTHERN STAR

FINISHED BLOCK: 16" × 16"

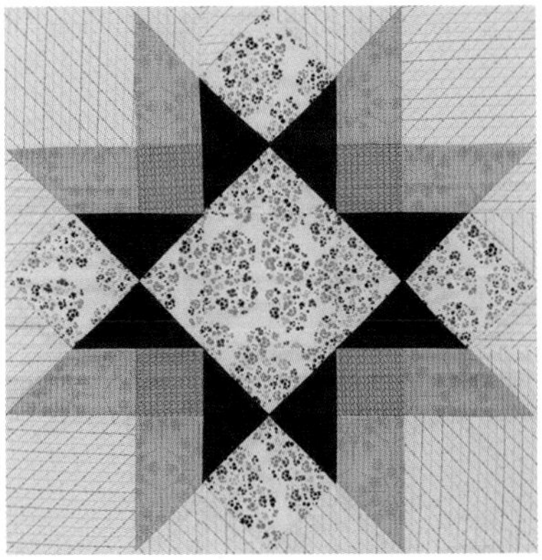

Materials

Materials are for making 2 identical blocks needed for the Barn Star Sampler. If you are making a different quilt, refer to the materials list for that project.

- ⅜ yard of light gray print #1 for background (fabric 27)
- 1 fat quarter of green print #2 for corner units (fabric 13)
- 1 square, 10" × 10", of teal print for corner units (fabric 19)
- 1 fat quarter of indigo print for side units (fabric 22)
- ⅜ yard of aqua floral #1 for side units and center square (fabric 14)

Cutting for 1 Block

The instructions yield pieces needed to make 1 block. Check the instructions for the project you're making to see how many blocks are needed. Label your pieces as you cut. The assembly diagrams refer to each piece by the letter that follows the dimensions.

From light gray print #1, cut:
4 □ 4½" × 4½" (A)
16 □ 2½" × 2½" (D)

From green print #2, cut:
8 ▭ 2½" × 4½" (B)

From the teal print, cut:
4 □ 2½" × 2½" (C)

From the indigo print, cut:
16 □ 2½" × 2½" (E)

From aqua floral #1, cut:
5 □ 4½" × 4½" (F)
4 ▭ 2½" × 4½" (G)

Making the Corner Units

Instructions are for making one block. Press seam allowances as indicated by the arrows.

1. Arrange one A square, two B pieces, and one C square in two rows. Sew all the pieces into rows and then join the rows. Make four units measuring 6½" square.

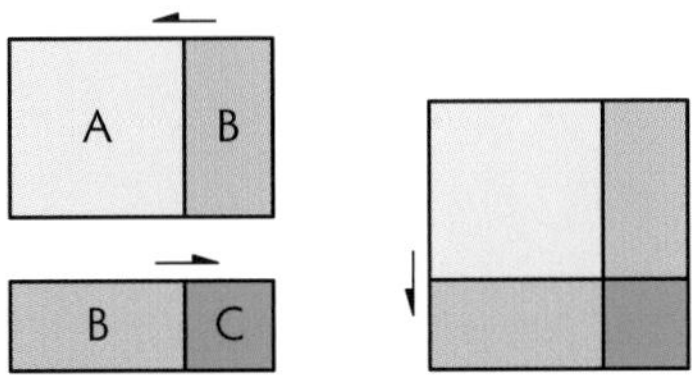

Make 4 units, 6½" × 6½".

2. Sew D squares to the upper-right and lower-left corners of a unit from step 1 (see page 74). Make four corner units measuring 6½" square.

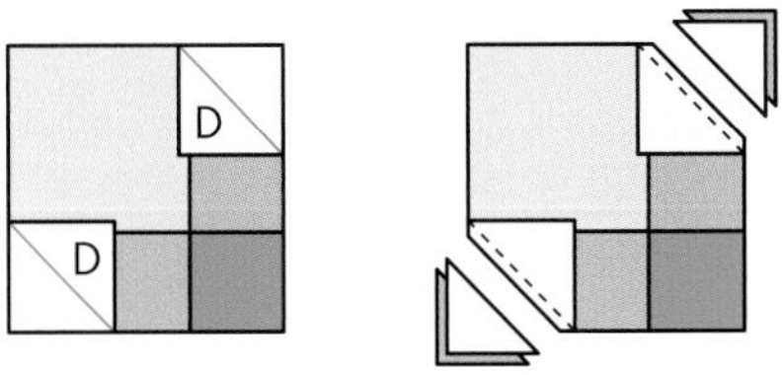

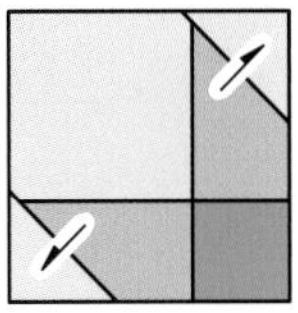
Make 4 units, 6½" × 6½".

Making the Side Units

1. Use D, E, and F squares to make four square-in-a-square units (see page 76) measuring 4½" square.

Make 4 units, 4½" × 4½".

2. Use E squares and G pieces to make four flying-geese units (see page 75) measuring 2½" × 4½".

Make 4 units, 2½" × 4½".

3. Join one unit each from steps 1 and 2. Make four side units measuring 4½" × 6½".

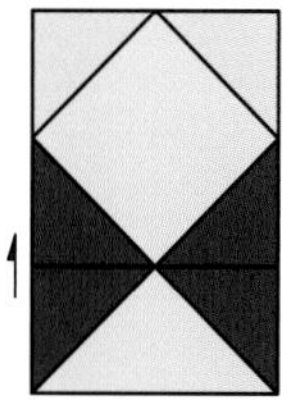

Make 4 units,
4½" × 6½".

Assembling Block 5

Arrange four corner units, four side units, and one F square in three rows. Sew all the pieces into rows and then join the rows. Make one block measuring 16½" square.

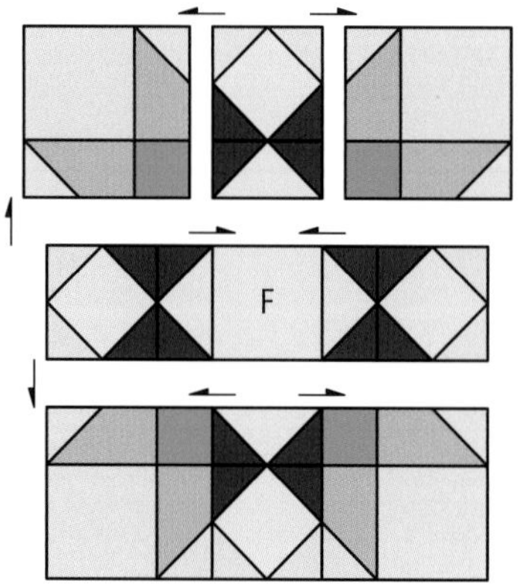

Make 1 block,
16½" × 16½".

BLOCK 6

MOROCCAN STAR

FINISHED BLOCK: 16" × 16"

Materials

Materials are for making 2 identical blocks needed for the Barn Star Sampler. If you are making a different quilt, refer to the materials list for that project.

 1 fat eighth of indigo print for corner units and center square (fabric 22)

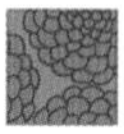 1 fat quarter of teal floral for corner and side units (fabric 20)

 1 fat quarter of white print #2 for corner and side units (fabric 26)

 1 fat quarter of aqua print for side units (fabric 17)

 1 fat eighth of light gray print #2 for side units (fabric 28)

Cutting for 1 Block

The instructions yield pieces needed to make 1 block. Check the instructions for the project you're making to see how many blocks are needed. Label your pieces as you cut. The assembly diagrams refer to each piece by the letter that follows the dimensions.

From the indigo print, cut:
4 □ 2½" × 2½" (A)
1 □ 4½" × 4½" (J)

From the teal floral, cut:
4 □ 2½" × 2½" (B)
4 ▭ 2½" × 4½" (C)
4 □ 4½" × 4½" (H)

From white print #2, cut:
4 ▭ 2½" × 4½" (D)
4 ▭ 2½" × 6½" (E)
8 □ 2½" × 2½" (G)

From the aqua print, cut:
16 □ 2½" × 2½" (F)

From light gray print #2, cut:
4 ▭ 2½" × 4½" (I)

Making the Corner Units

Instructions are for making one block. Press seam allowances as indicated by the arrows.

Join A and B squares. Then add C, D, and E pieces to make four corner units measuring 6½" square.

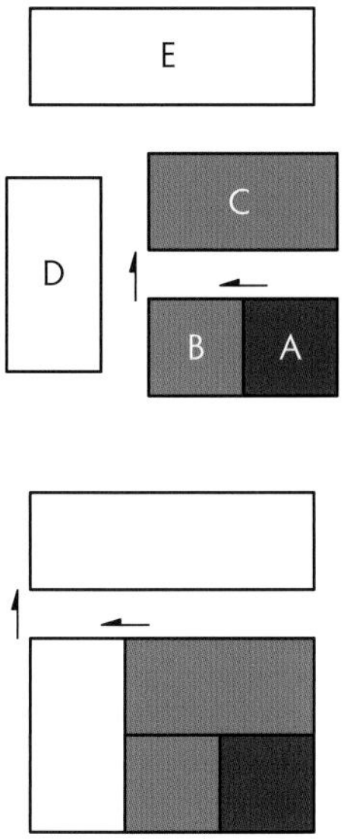

Make 4 units,
6½" × 6½".

Making the Side Units

1. Use F, G, and H squares to make four square-in-a-square units (see page 76) measuring 4½" square.

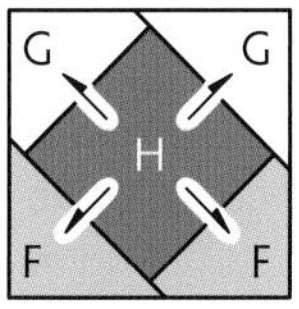

Make 4 units,
4½" × 4½".

2. Use F squares and I pieces to make four flying-geese units (see page 75) measuring 2½" × 4½".

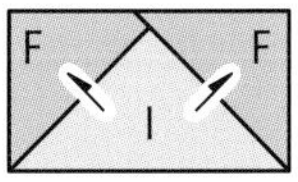

Make 4 units,
2½" × 4½".

3. Join one of each unit from steps 1 and 2 to make four side units measuring 4½" × 6½".

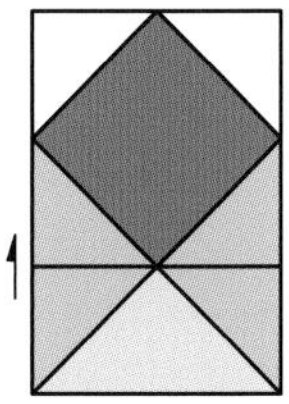

Make 4 units,
4½" × 6½".

Assembling Block 6

Arrange four corner units, four side units, and one J square in three rows. Sew all the pieces into rows and then join the rows. Make one block measuring 16½" square.

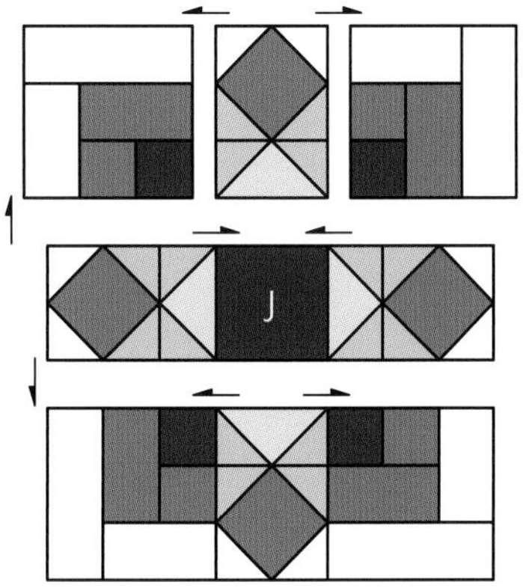

Make 1 block,
16½" × 16½".

BLOCK 7

FRIENDSHIP STAR

FINISHED BLOCK: 16" × 16"

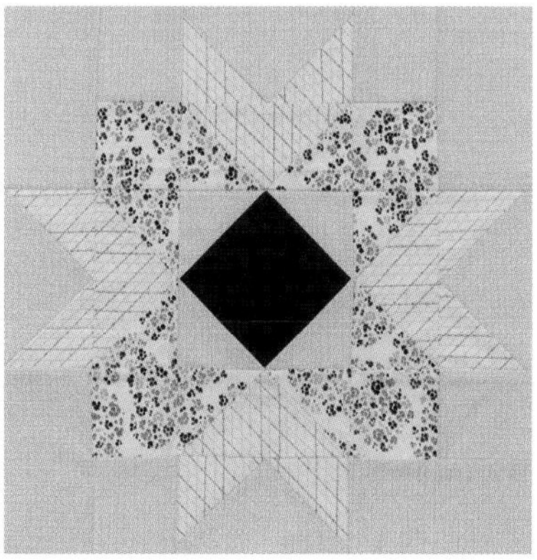

Materials

Materials are for making 2 identical blocks needed for the Barn Star Sampler.

1 fat quarter of aqua floral #1 for corner and side units (fabric 14)

⅝ yard of light aqua print for background (fabric 16)

⅜ yard of light gray print #1 for side units (fabric 27)

1 fat eighth of indigo print for center units (fabric 22)

Cutting for 1 Block

The instructions yield pieces needed to make 1 block. Check the instructions for the project you're making to see how many blocks are needed. Label your pieces as you cut. The assembly diagrams refer to each piece by the letter that follows the dimensions.

From aqua floral #1, cut:
12 □ 3" × 3" (A)

From the light aqua print, cut:
4 ▭ 3" × 3½" (B)
4 ▭ 3½" × 6" (C)
4 ▭ 3½" × 5½" (F)
4 □ 3" × 3" (G)

From light gray print #1, cut:
4 ▭ 3" × 5½" (D)
8 □ 3" × 3" (E)

From the indigo print, cut:
1 □ 5½" × 5½" (H)

Making the Corner Units

Instructions are for making one block. Press seam allowances as indicated by the arrows.

Join an A square and a B piece. Sew a C piece to the top edge. Make four corner units measuring 6" square.

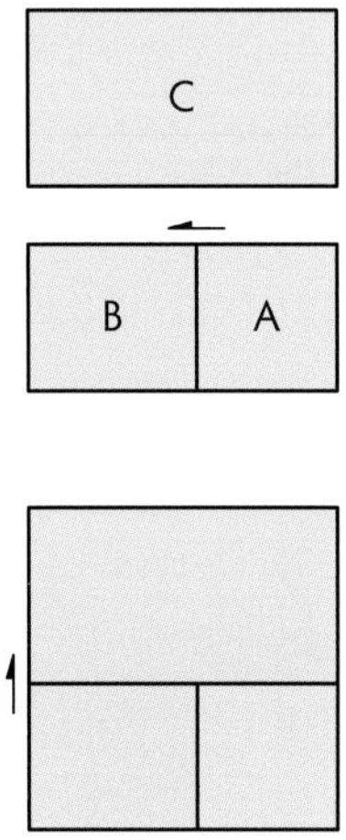

Make 4 units,
6" × 6".

Making the Side Units

1. Use A squares and D pieces to make four flying-geese units (see page 75) measuring 3" × 5½".

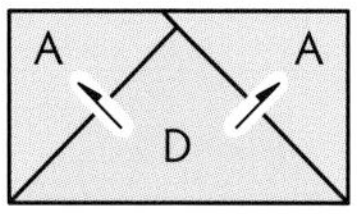

Make 4 units,
3" × 5½".

2. Use E squares and F pieces to make four house units (see page 75) measuring 3½" × 5½".

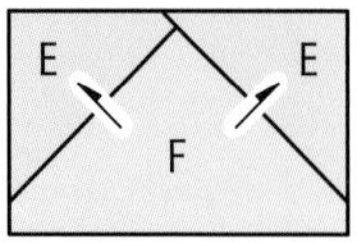

Make 4 units,
3½" × 5½".

3. Join one of each unit from steps 1 and 2 as shown. Make four side units measuring 5½" × 6".

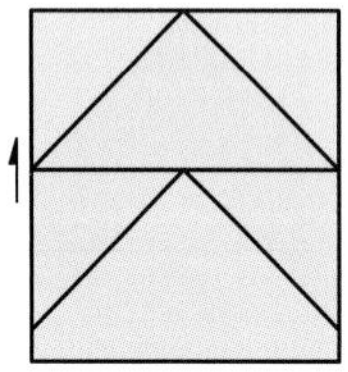

Make 4 units,
5½" × 6".

Making the Center Units

Use G and H squares to make one square-in-a-square unit (see page 76) measuring 5½" square.

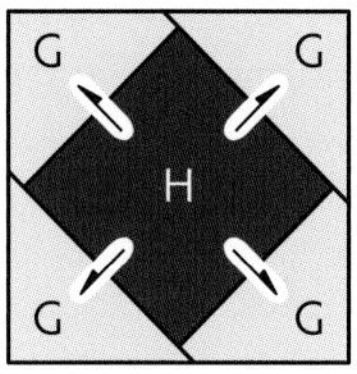

Make 1 unit,
5½" × 5½".

Assembling Block 7

Arrange four corner units, four side units, and one center unit in three rows. Sew the units into rows and then join the rows. Make one block measuring 16½" square.

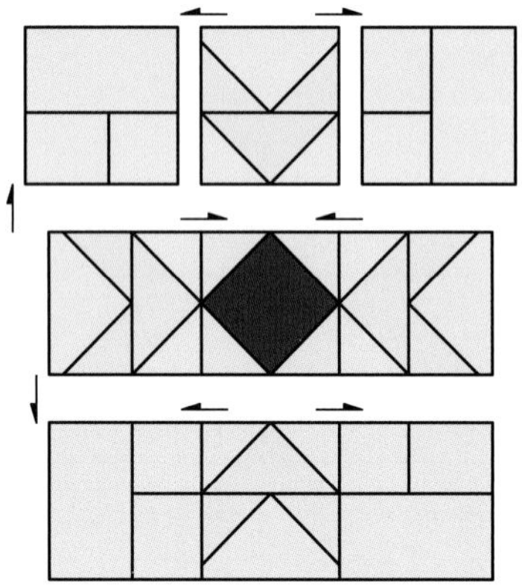

Make 1 block,
16½" × 16½".

BLOCK 8

FARMER'S STAR

FINISHED BLOCK: 16" × 16"

Materials

Materials are for making 2 identical blocks needed for the Barn Star Sampler. If you are making a different quilt, refer to the materials list for that project.

 1 fat eighth of green print #1 for corner units (fabric 12)

 ⅜ yard of white print #1 for background (fabric 25)

 1 fat eighth of medium aqua print for corner and side units (fabric 18)

 1 fat quarter of indigo floral for side units (fabric 21)

 1 square, 10" × 10", of aqua floral #2 for center units (fabric 15)

 1 square, 10" × 10", of dark indigo print for center units (fabric 23)

Cutting for 1 Block

The instructions yield pieces needed to make 1 block. Check the instructions for the project you're making to see how many blocks are needed. Label your pieces as you cut. The assembly diagrams refer to each piece by the letter that follows the dimensions.

From green print #1, cut:
8 □ 2½" × 2½" (A)

From white print #1, cut:
12 ▭ 2½" × 4½" (B)
8 □ 2½" × 2½" (C)

From the medium aqua print, cut:
12 □ 2½" × 2½" (D)

From the indigo floral, cut:
4 □ 4½" × 4½" (E)
8 □ 2½" × 2½" (F)

From aqua floral #2, cut:
4 □ 2½" × 2½" (G)

From the dark indigo print, cut:
1 □ 4½" × 4½" (H)

Making the Corner Units

Instructions are for making one block. Press seam allowances as indicated by the arrows.

Arrange two A squares, two B pieces, two C squares, and one D square in three rows. Sew all the pieces into rows and then join the rows. Make four corner units measuring 6½" square.

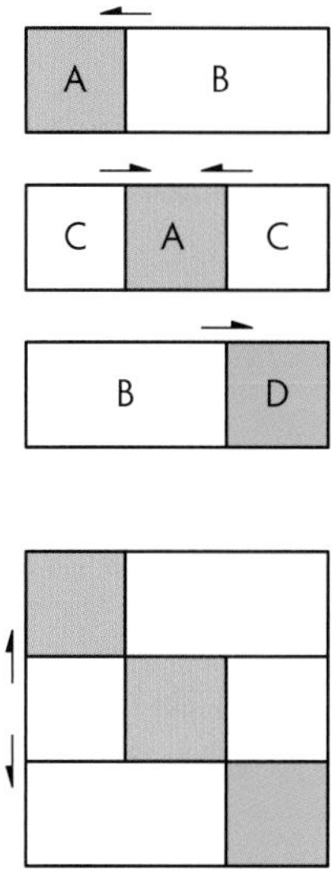

Make 4 units,
6½" × 6½".

Making the Side Units

1. Use D and E squares to make four house units (see page 75) measuring 4½" square.

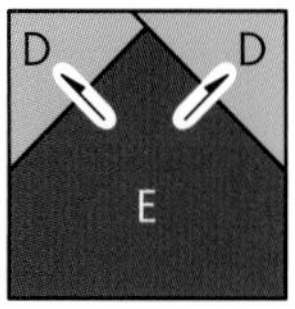

Make 4 units,
4½" × 4½".

2. Use F squares and B pieces to make four flying-geese units (see page 75) measuring 2½" × 4½".

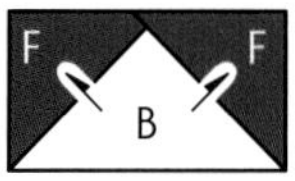

Make 4 units,
2½" × 4½".

3. Join one unit each from steps 1 and 2 as shown. Make four side units measuring 4½" × 6½".

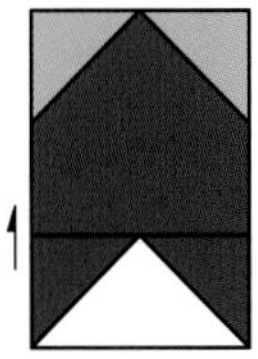

Make 4 units, 4½" × 6½".

Making the Center Units

Use G and H squares to make one square-in-a-square unit (see page 76) measuring 4½" square.

Make 1 unit, 4½" × 4½".

Assembling Block 8

Arrange four corner units, four side units, and one center unit in three rows. Join the units to make one block measuring 16½" square.

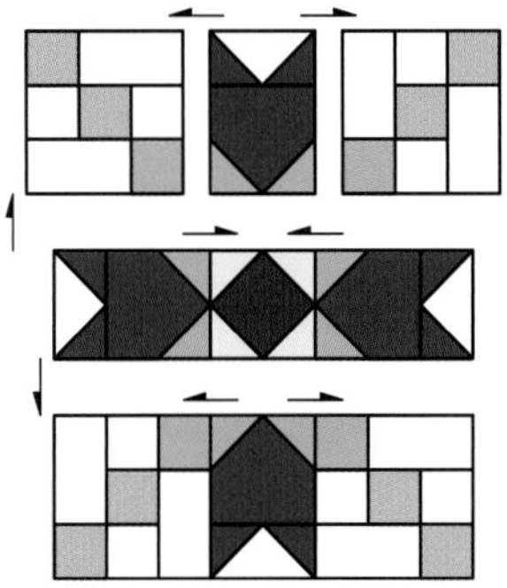

Make 1 block, 16½" × 16½".

BLOCK 9

PEONY STAR

FINISHED BLOCK: 16" × 16"

Materials

Materials are for making 2 identical blocks needed for the Barn Star Sampler. If you are making a different quilt, refer to the materials list for that project.

 ½ yard of white solid for background (fabric 24)

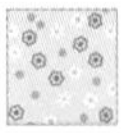 1 fat eighth of coral floral for corner units (fabric 3)

 1 fat quarter of dark raspberry floral for corner and side units (fabric 7)

 1 fat eighth of plum floral for corner units and center square (fabric 9)

 1 fat eighth of white-and-raspberry print for side units (fabric 1)

Cutting for 1 Block

The instructions yield pieces needed to make 1 block. Check instructions for the project you're making to see how many blocks are needed. Label pieces as you cut. The assembly diagrams refer to each piece by the letter that follows the dimensions.

From the white solid, cut:
4 □ 4" × 4" (A)
2 ▭ 1" × 15½" (I)
2 ▭ 1" × 16½" (J)
8 □ 2" × 2" (F)
4 ▭ 2" × 3½" (H)

From the coral floral, cut:
4 □ 4" × 4" (B)

From the dark raspberry floral, cut:
8 □ 3½" × 3½" (C)

From the plum floral, cut:
5 □ 3½" × 3½" (D)

From the white-and-raspberry print, cut:
8 □ 2" × 2" (E)
4 ▭ 2" × 3½" (G)

Making the Corner Units

Instructions are for making one block. Press seam allowances as indicated by the arrows.

1. Use A and B squares to make eight half-square-triangle units (see page 77) and trim them to 3½" square.

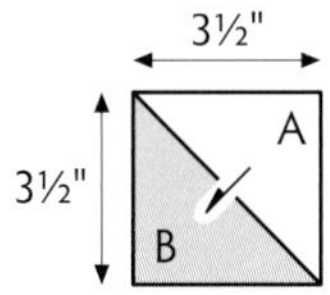

Make 8 units.

2. Arrange two triangle units, one C square, and one D square in two rows. Sew all the pieces into rows and then join the rows. Make four corner units measuring 6½" square.

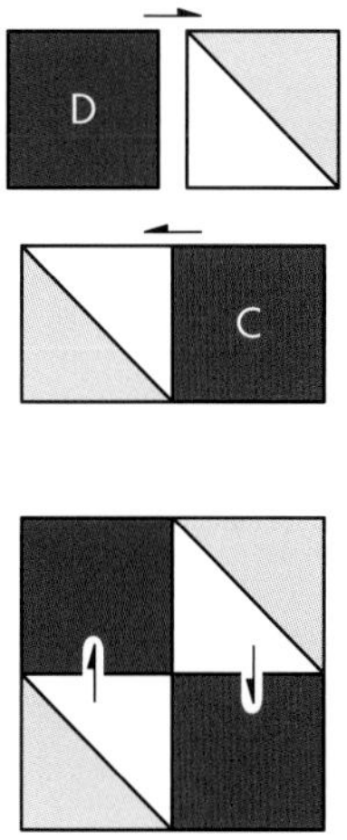

Make 4 units,
6½" × 6½".

Making the Side Units

1. Use C, E, and F squares to make four square-in-a-square units (see page 76) measuring 3½" square.

Make 4 units,
3½" × 3½".

2. Sew a G piece to the bottom and an H piece to the top of a unit from step 1. Make four side units measuring 3½" × 6½".

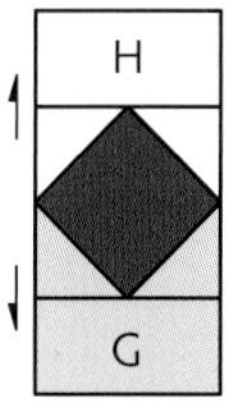

Make 4 units,
3½" × 6½".

Assembling Block 9

1. Arrange four corner units, four side units, and one D square in three rows. Sew all the pieces into rows and then join the rows. Make one unit measuring 15½" square.

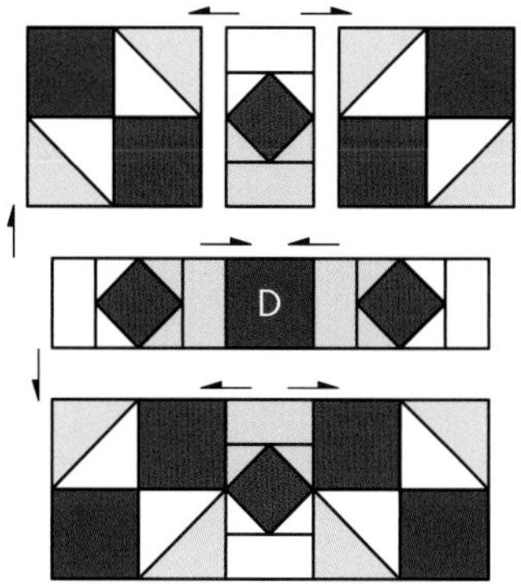

Make 1 unit,
15½" × 15½".

2. Sew one I strip to the left and one I strip to the right edge of a unit from step 1. Sew J strips to the top and bottom edges. Make one block measuring 16½" square.

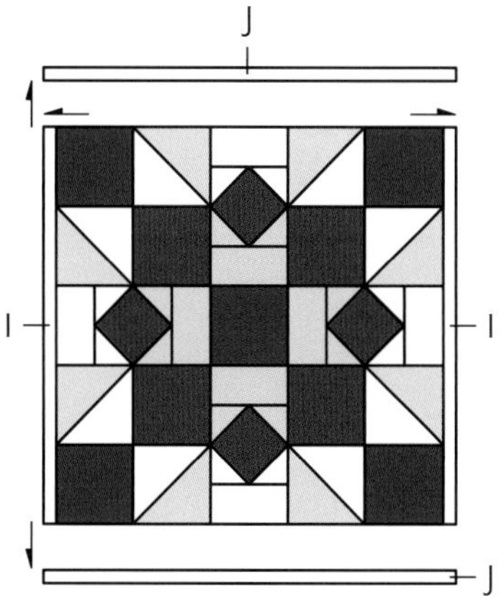

Make 1 block,
16½" × 16½".

BLOCK 10

RIBBON STAR

FINISHED BLOCK: 8" × 8"

Materials

Materials are for making 3 identical blocks needed for the Barn Star Sampler.

 1 fat quarter of raspberry floral for flying-geese and square-in-a-square units (fabric 5)

 1 fat quarter of light gold floral for background (fabric 10)

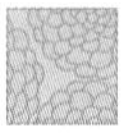 1 square, 10" × 10", of gold floral for square-in-a-square units (fabric 11)

Cutting for 1 Block

The instructions yield pieces needed to make 1 block. Check the instructions for the project you're making to see how many blocks are needed. Label your pieces as you cut. The assembly diagrams refer to each piece by the letter that follows the dimensions.

From the raspberry floral, cut:
12 ☐ 2½" × 2½" (A)

From the light gold floral, cut:
4 ▭ 2½" × 4½" (B)
4 ☐ 2½" × 2½" (D)

From the gold floral, cut:
1 ☐ 4½" × 4½" (C)

Assembling Block 10

Instructions are for making one block. Press seam allowances as indicated by the arrows.

1. Use A squares and B pieces to make four flying-geese units (see page 75) measuring 2½" × 4½".

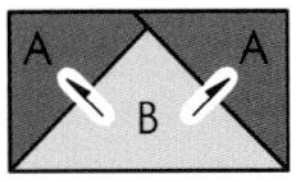

Make 4 units, 2½" × 4½".

2. Use A and C squares to make one square-in-a-square unit (see page 76) measuring 4½" square.

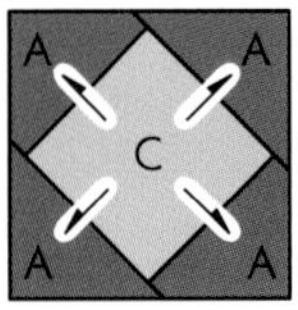

Make 1 unit, 4½" × 4½".

3. Arrange four units from step 1, one unit from step 2, and four D squares in three rows. Sew all the pieces into rows and then join the rows. Make one block measuring 8½" square.

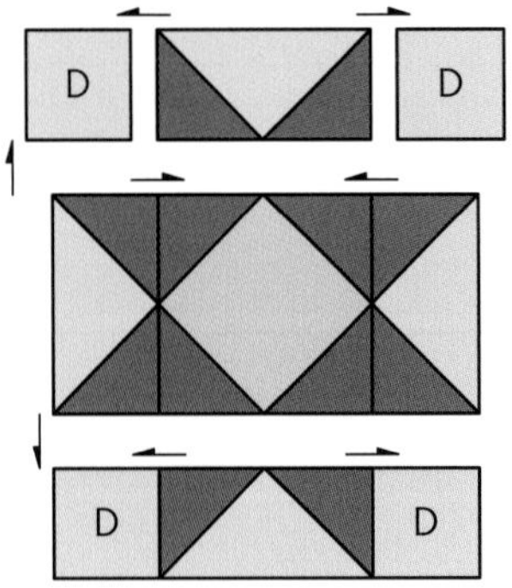

Make 1 block, 8½" × 8½".

BLOCK 11

MOSAIC STAR

FINISHED BLOCK: 8" × 8"

Materials

Materials are for making 3 identical blocks needed for the Barn Star Sampler. If you are making a different quilt, refer to the materials list for that project.

 1 fat eighth of white-and-raspberry print for half-square-triangle and square-in-a-square units (fabric 1)

 1 fat eighth of coral print for half-square-triangle and square-in-a-square units (fabric 4)

 1 fat eighth of plum floral for flying-geese units (fabric 9)

 1 fat eighth of light gray print #2 for flying-geese units (fabric 28)

Cutting for 1 Block

The instructions yield pieces needed to make 1 block. Check the instructions for the project you're making to see how many blocks are needed. Label your pieces as you cut. The assembly diagrams refer to each piece by the letter that follows the dimensions.

From the white-and-raspberry print, cut:
2 □ 3" × 3" (A)
4 □ 2½" × 2½" (E)

From the coral print, cut:
2 □ 3" × 3" (B)
1 □ 4½" × 4½" (F)

From the plum floral, cut:
8 □ 2½" × 2½" (C)

From the light gray print #2, cut:
4 ▭ 2½" × 4½" (D)

Assembling Block 11

Instructions are for making one block. Press seam allowances as indicated by the arrows.

1. Use A and B squares to make four half-square-triangle units (see page77) and trim them to 2½" square.

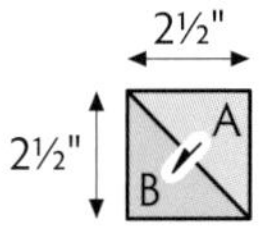

Make 4 units.

2. Use C squares and D pieces to make four flying-geese units (see page 75) measuring 2½" × 4½".

Make 4 units,
2½" × 4½".

3. Use E and F squares to make one square-in-a-square unit (see page 76) measuring 4½" square.

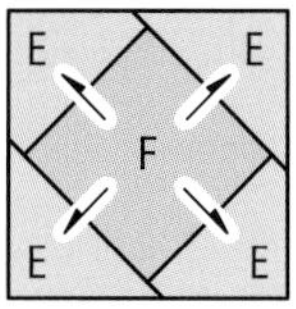

Make 1 unit,
4½" × 4½".

4. Arrange four units each from steps 1 and 2 and one unit from step 3 in three rows. Sew the units into rows and then join the rows. Make one block measuring 8½" square.

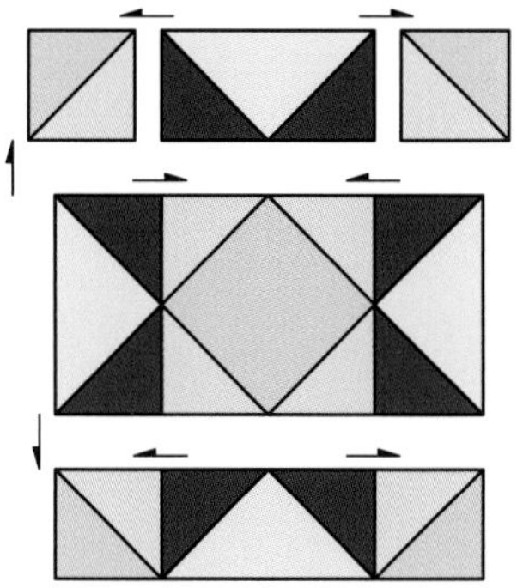

Make 1 block,
8½" × 8½".

BLOCK 12

OHIO STAR

FINISHED BLOCK: 8" × 8"

Materials

Materials are for making 3 identical blocks needed for the Barn Star Sampler. If you are making a different quilt, refer to the materials list for that project.

 1 fat eighth of indigo floral for hourglass units (fabric 21)

 1 square, 10" × 10", of white print #1 for hourglass units (fabric 25)

 1 fat quarter of coral print for background (fabric 4)

 1 square, 10" × 10", of light gold floral for center square (fabric 10)

Cutting for 1 Block

The instructions yield pieces needed to make 1 block. Check the instructions for the project you're making to see how many blocks are needed. Label your pieces as you cut. The assembly diagrams refer to each piece by the letter that follows the dimensions.

From the indigo floral, cut:
2 ⊠ 3½" × 3½"(A)

From white print #1, cut:
1 ⊠ 3½" × 3½" (B)

From the coral print, cut:
1 ⊠ 3½" × 3½" (C)
4 □ 3½" × 3½" (E)
4 ▭ 1½" × 2½" (D)

From the light gold floral, cut:
1 □ 2½" × 2½" (F)

Assembling Block 12

Instructions are for making one block. Press seam allowances as indicated by the arrows.

1. Join A, B, and C triangles to make four hourglass units and trim them to 2½" square (see page 77).

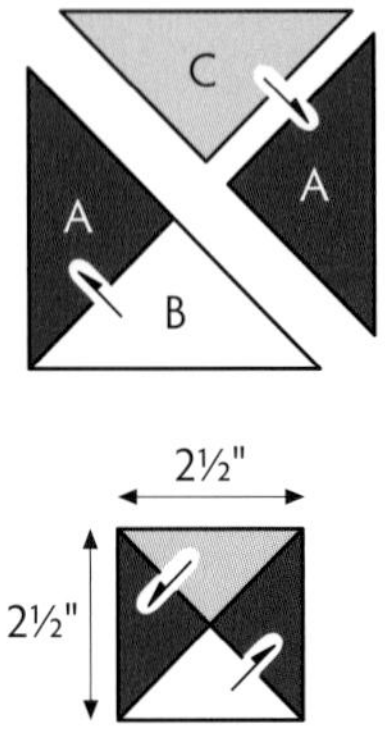

Make 4 units.

2. Sew a D piece to the top of each hourglass unit to make four units measuring 2½" × 3½".

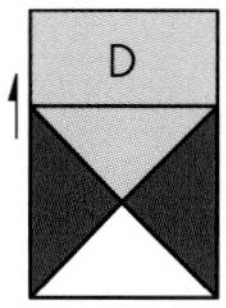

Make 4 units,
2½" × 3½".

3. Arrange four units from step 2, four E squares, and one F square in three rows. Sew the pieces into rows and then join the rows. Make one block measuring 8½" square.

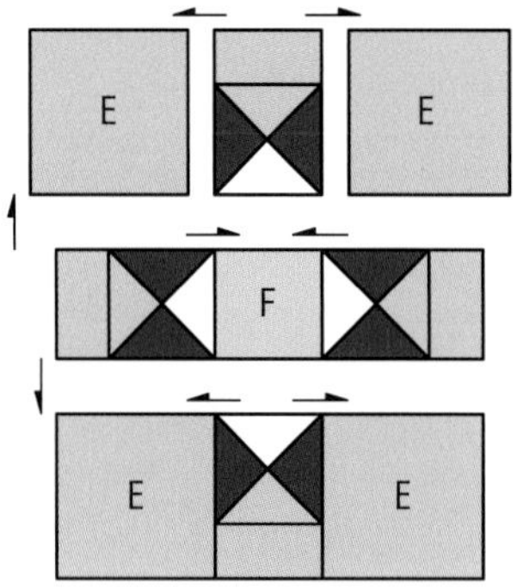

Make 1 block,
8½" × 8½".

BLOCK 13
WEATHERVANE STAR

FINISHED BLOCK: 8" × 8"

Materials

Materials are for making 3 identical blocks needed for the Barn Star Sampler. If you are making a different quilt, refer to the materials list for that project.

 1 fat eighth of green print #2 for corner units (fabric 13)

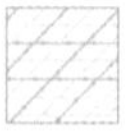 1 fat quarter of light gray print #1 for background (fabric 27)

 1 fat eighth of aqua print for side units (fabric 17)

 1 square, 10" × 10", of dark indigo print for center square (fabric 23)

Cutting for 1 Block

The instructions yield pieces needed to make 1 block. Check the instructions for the project you're making to see how many blocks are needed. Label your pieces as you cut. The assembly diagrams refer to each piece by the letter that follows the dimensions.

From green print #2, cut:
4 □ 1½" × 1½" (A)
4 ▭ 1½" × 2½" (C)

From light gray print #1, cut:
12 ▭ 1½" × 2½" (B)
4 □ 2½" × 2½" (D)
8 □ 1½" × 1½" (E)

From the aqua print, cut:
4 □ 2½" × 2½" (F)

From the dark indigo print, cut:
1 □ 2½" × 2½" (G)

Making the Corner Units

Instructions are for making one block. Press seam allowances as indicated by the arrows.

1. Sew an A square to the right end of a B piece (see page 74). Make four units measuring 1½" × 2½".

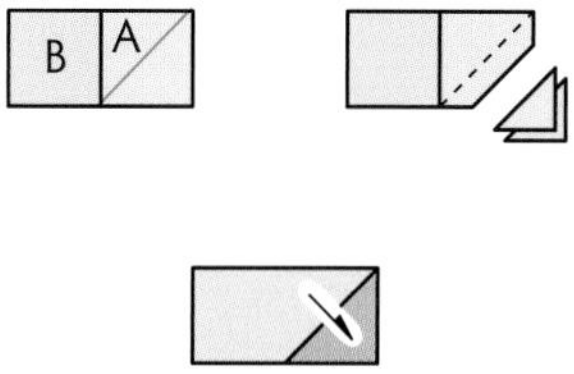

Make 4 units, 1½" × 2½".

2. Sew a C piece to the right end of a B piece as shown (see page 76). Make four units measuring 1½" × 3½".

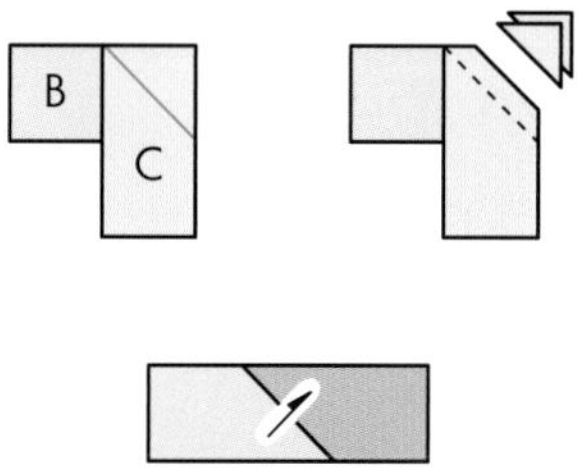

Make 4 units, 1½" × 3½".

3. Sew a unit from step 1 to a D square. Sew a unit from step 2 to the bottom edge. Make four corner units measuring 3½" square.

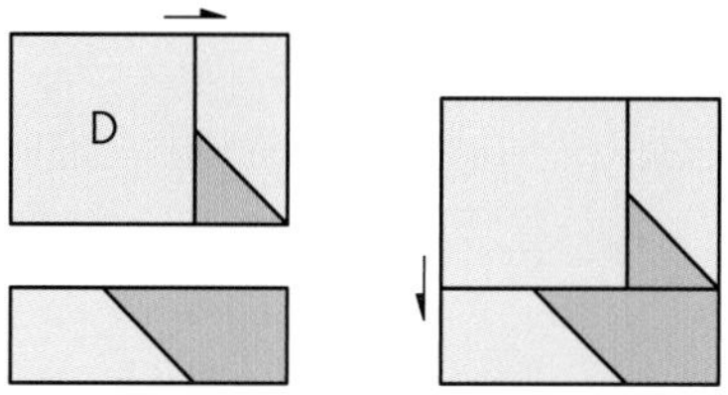

Make 4 units, 3½" × 3½".

Making the Side Units

1. Use E and F squares to make four house units (see page 75). The units should measure 2½" square.

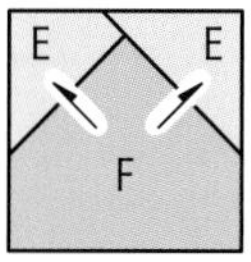

Make 4 units, 2½" × 2½".

2. Sew a B piece to the top of a house unit. Make four side units measuring 2½" × 3½".

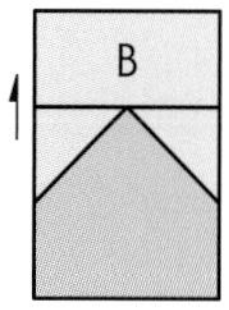

Make 4 units, 2½" × 3½".

Assembling Block 13

Arrange four corner units, four side units, and one G square in three rows. Sew the pieces into rows and then join the rows. Make one block measuring 8½" square.

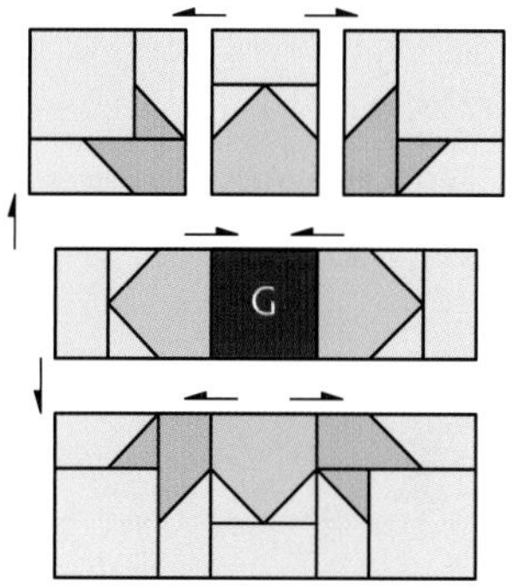

Make 1 block, 8½" × 8½".

BLOCK 14

PINWHEEL STAR

FINISHED BLOCK: 8" × 8"

Materials

Materials are for making 3 identical blocks needed for the Barn Star Sampler.

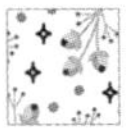 1 fat quarter of white-and-raspberry print for background (fabric 1)

 1 fat eighth of plum floral for block (fabric 9)

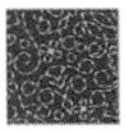 1 fat eighth of raspberry floral for block (fabric 5)

Cutting for 1 Block

The instructions yield pieces needed to make 1 block. Check the instructions for the project you're making to see how many blocks are needed. Label your pieces as you cut. The assembly diagrams refer to each piece by the letter that follows the dimensions.

From the white-and-raspberry print, cut:
2 □ 3" × 3" (A)
8 □ 2½" × 2½" (C)

From the plum floral, cut:
2 □ 3" × 3" (B)
4 □ 2½" × 2½" (E)

From the raspberry floral, cut:
4 ▭ 2½" × 4½" (D)

Assembling Block 14

Instructions are for making one block. Press seam allowances as indicated by the arrows.

1. Use A and B squares to make four half-square-triangle units (see page 77) and trim them to 2½" square.

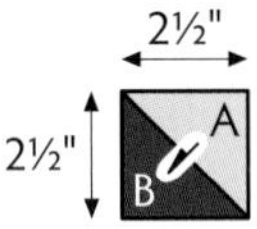

Make 4 units.

2. Sew a C square to the left end of a D piece (see page 74). Sew an E square to the right end. Make four units measuring 2½" × 4½".

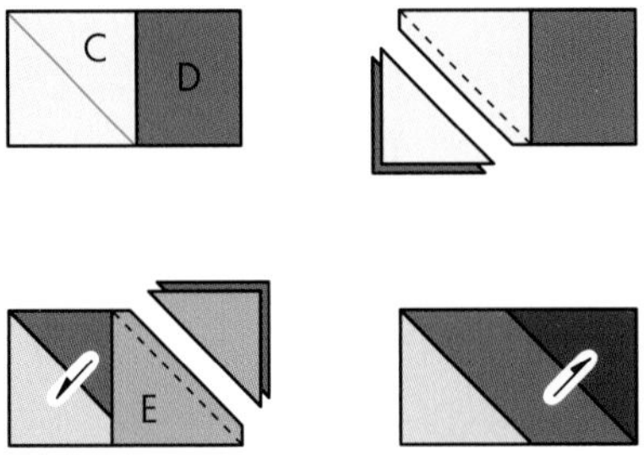

Make 4 units, 2½" × 4½".

3. Sew a unit from step 1 to a C square, then sew a unit from step 2 to the bottom edge. Make four units measuring 4½" square.

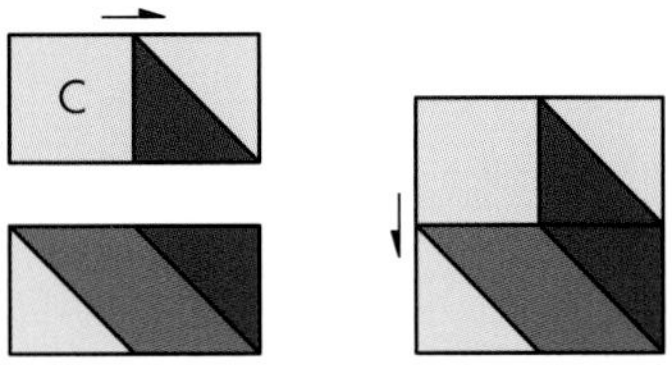

Make 4 units, 4½" × 4½".

4. Arrange four units from step 3 in two rows. Sew the units into rows and then join the rows. Press seam allowances in a clockwise direction (page 18). Make one block measuring 8½" square.

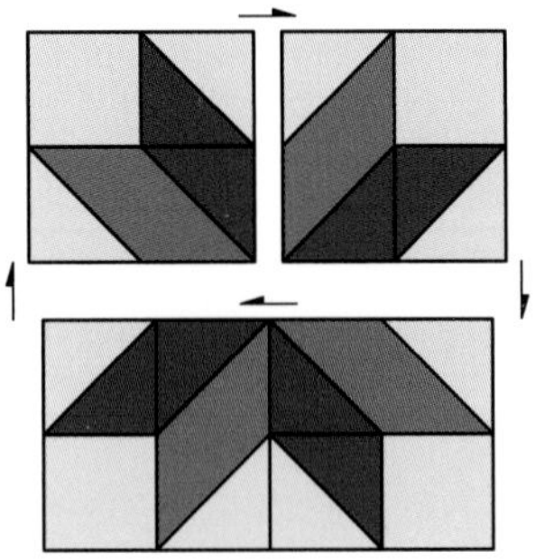

Make 1 block, 8½" × 8½".

BLOCK 15

WINDMILL STAR

FINISHED BLOCK: 8" × 8"

Materials

Materials are for making 3 blocks needed for the Barn Star Sampler. If you are making a different quilt, refer to the materials list for that project.

 1 fat eighth of indigo floral for corner units (fabric 21)

 1 fat quarter of white print #1 for background (fabric 25)

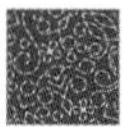 1 square, 10" × 10", of raspberry floral for side units (fabric 5)

 1 square, 10" × 10", of dark raspberry print for side units (fabric 8)

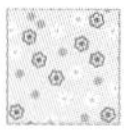 1 square, 10" × 10", of coral floral for center square (fabric 3)

Cutting for 1 Block

The instructions yield pieces needed to make 1 block. Check the instructions for the project you're making to see how many blocks are needed. Label your pieces as you cut. The assembly diagrams refer to each piece by the letter that follows the dimensions.

From the indigo floral, cut:
12 ☐ 1½" × 1½" (A)

From the white print #1, cut:
12 ▭ 1½" × 2½" (B)
8 ☐ 1½" × 1½" (C)
1 ⊠ 3½" × 3½" (D)

From the raspberry floral, cut:
1 ⊠ 3½" × 3½" (E)

From the dark raspberry print, cut:
2 ◩ 3" × 3" (F)

From the coral floral, cut:
1 ☐ 2½" × 2½" (G)

Assembling Block 15

Instructions are for making one block. Press seam allowances as indicated by the arrows.

1. Arrange three A squares, two B pieces, and two C squares in three rows. Join the pieces to make four corner units measuring 3½" square.

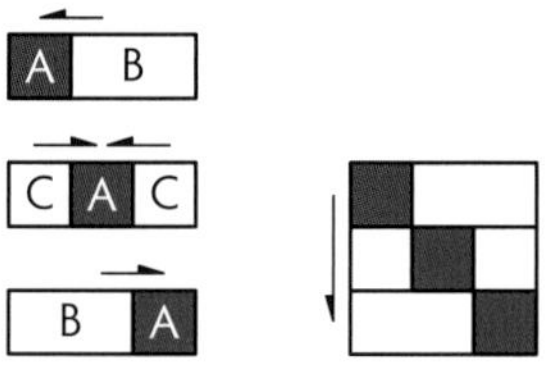

Make 4 units, 3½" × 3½".

2. Join D, E, and F triangles as shown. Make four units and trim them to 2½" square.

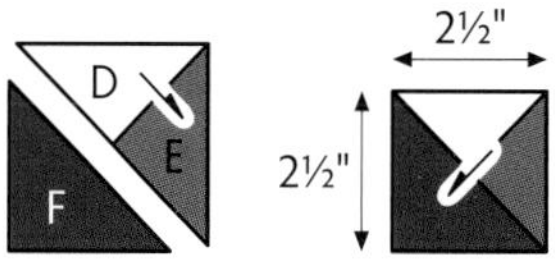

Make 4 units.

3. Sew a B piece to the top of a unit from step 2. Make four units measuring 2½" × 3½".

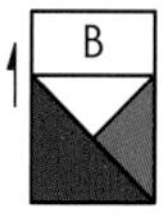

Make 4 units, 2½" × 3½".

4. Arrange four corner units, four side units, and one G square in three rows. Join the pieces to make one block measuring 8½" square.

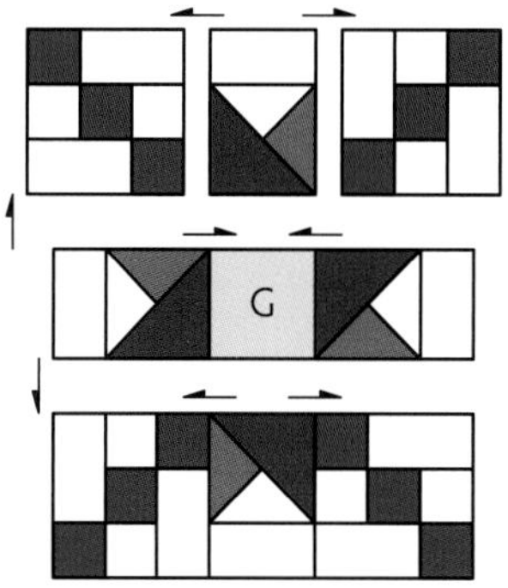

Make 1 block, 8½" × 8½".

MAKE IT YOUR OWN

Blocks 16–20 are a little bit different from the previous blocks. These tiny 4" blocks are meant to function as "blender blocks" in the sampler, helping to balance out the colors and prints used in the larger blocks. Rather than making identical sets of blocks, use a variety of prints to give them a scrappy feel.

In the quilt shown (page 38), I used ¼ yard of fabric 26 for the background in many of the 4" blocks. The rest of the prints and background fabrics were sourced from the scraps left over from piecing the larger blocks. I've labeled the exact prints I used in my sampler quilt, but feel free to mix and match your own prints and make the blocks as scrappy or planned as you'd like!

BLOCK 16

SAWTOOTH STAR

FINISHED BLOCK: 4" × 4"

Materials

Materials are for making 4 blocks needed for the Barn Star Sampler. If you are making a different quilt, refer to the materials list for that project. **Note:** *Three of the blocks in my sampler were made using fabrics 6 or 9 as the focal prints, with fabric 26 as the background. The fourth block was made using fabric 22 as the focal print and fabric 17 as the background.*

¼ yard *total* of assorted print scraps for star (fabrics 6, 9, and 22)

1 fat eighth of white print #2 for background (fabric 26)

5" × 7" piece of aqua print for background (fabric 17)

Cutting for 1 Block

The instructions yield pieces to make 1 block. Check instructions for the project you're making to see how many blocks are needed. Label the pieces as you cut. The assembly diagrams refer to each piece by the letter that follows the dimensions.

From the assorted print scraps, cut a matching set of:

8 □ 1½" × 1½" (A)
1 □ 2½" × 2½" (D)

From white print #2 or the aqua print, cut a matching set of:

4 ▭ 1½" × 2½" (B)
4 □ 1½" × 1½" (C)

Assembling Block 16

Press seam allowances as indicated by the arrows.

1. Use A squares and B pieces to make four flying-geese units (page 75) measuring 1½" × 2½".

Make 4 units, 1½" × 2½".

2. Join the flying-geese units and C and D squares. Make one block measuring 4½" square.

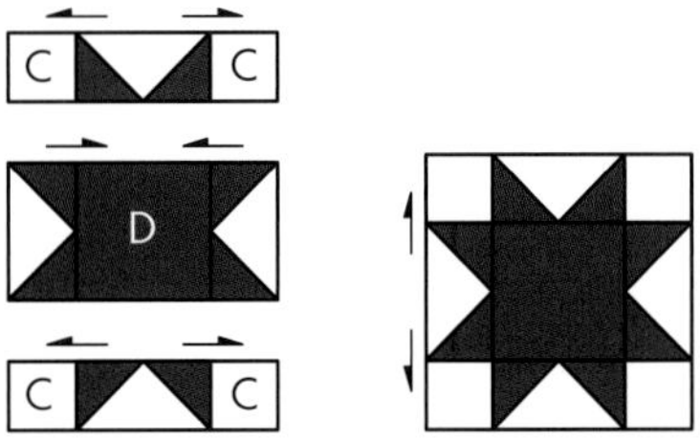

Make 1 block, 4½" × 4½".

BLOCK 17

FLYING GEESE

FINISHED BLOCK: 4" × 4"

Materials

Materials are for making 4 blocks for the Barn Star Sampler. If you are making a different quilt, refer to the materials list for that project. I made 2 blocks using fabrics 15 or 16 for background and fabrics 21 or 23 as the main print or "geese." The other 2 blocks were made using fabrics 7 and 28 for the background, and fabrics 3 or 4 as the geese. All fabrics are scraps of previous blocks.

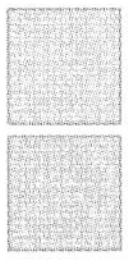

1 fat eighth *total* of assorted print scraps for background (fabrics 7, 15, 16, and 28)

1 fat eighth *total* of assorted print scraps for geese (fabrics 3, 4, 21, and 23)

Cutting for 1 Block

The instructions yield pieces needed to make 1 block. Check the instructions for your project to see how many blocks are needed. Label pieces as you cut. The assembly diagrams refer to each piece by the letter that follows the dimensions.

From 1 of the prints for the background, cut:
2 □ 2½" × 2½" (A)

From a different print for the background, cut:
2 □ 2½" × 2½" (A)

From 1 of the prints for the geese, cut:
1 ▭ 2½" × 4½" (B)

From a different print for the geese, cut:
1 ▭ 2½" × 4½" (B)

Assembling Block 17

Press seam allowances as indicated by the arrows.

1. Use A squares and B pieces to make two flying-geese units (see page 75) measuring 2½" × 4½".

Make 1 unit, 2½" × 4½".

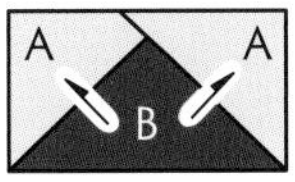

Make 1 unit, 2½" × 4½".

2. Join the units from step 1 to make a block. Make one block measuring 4½" square.

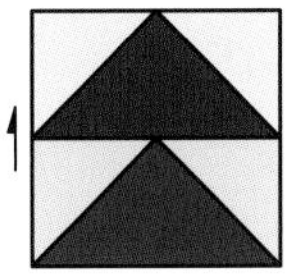

Make 1 block, 4½" × 4½".

BLOCK 18

WHIRLIGIGS

FINISHED BLOCK: 4" × 4"

Materials

Materials are for making 4 blocks needed for the Barn Star Sampler. If you are making a different quilt, refer to the materials list for that project. I made 1 block using fabrics 15 and 23, 1 block using fabrics 10 and 11, and 2 blocks using fabrics 20 and 26. All fabrics are scraps of previous blocks.

1 fat eighth *total* of assorted scraps for background (fabrics 10, 15, and 26)

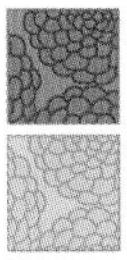

1 fat eighth *total* of assorted scraps for pinwheel (fabrics 11, 20, and 23)

Cutting for 1 Block

The instructions yield pieces needed for 1 block. Check the instructions for the project you're making to see how many blocks are needed. Label pieces as you cut. The assembly diagrams refer to each piece by the letter that follows the dimensions.

From 1 print for background, cut:
2 ◻ 3" × 3" (A)

From 1 print for pinwheel, cut:
2 ◻ 3" × 3" (B)

Assembling Block 18

Press seam allowances as indicated by the arrows.

1. Use A and B squares to make four half-square-triangle units (see page 77) and trim them to 2½" square.

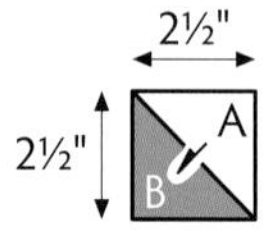

Make 4 units.

2. Lay out the triangle units in two rows. Join the units and press seam allowances in a counterclockwise direction (page 18). Make one block measuring 4½" square.

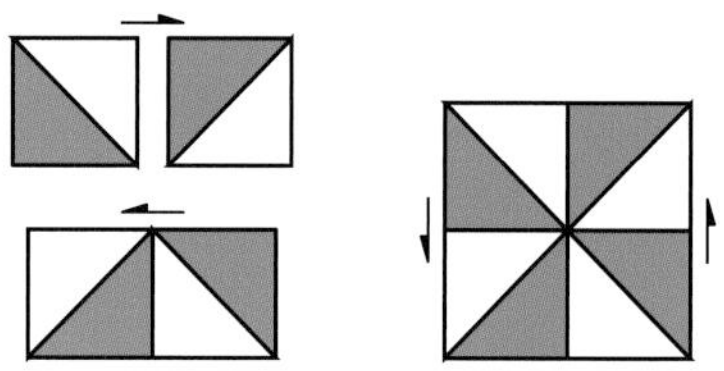

Make 1 block, 4½" × 4½".

BLOCK 19

MILL WHEELS

FINISHED BLOCK: 4" × 4"

Materials

Materials are for making 4 blocks needed for the Barn Star Sampler. If you are making a different quilt, refer to the materials list for that project. I used fabrics 15, 17, 18, and 19 as focal prints, and fabric 26 as the background print in each block.

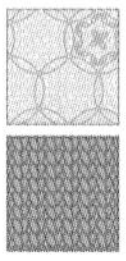

1 fat quarter *total* of assorted aqua prints for block (fabrics 15, 17, 18, and 19)

1 fat eighth of white print #2 for block backgrounds (fabric 26)

Cutting for 1 Block

The instructions yield pieces needed to make 1 block. Check the instructions for the project you're making to see how many blocks are needed. Label your pieces as you cut. The assembly diagrams refer to each piece by the letter that follows the dimensions.

From 1 of the aqua prints, cut a matching set of:
4 ◻ 1½" × 1½" (A)
4 ▭ 1½" × 2½" (C)
1 ◻ 2½" × 2½" (E)

From white print #2, cut:
4 ▭ 1½" × 2½" (B)
4 ◻ 1½" × 1½" (D)

Assembling Block 19

Press seam allowances as indicated by the arrows.

1. Use A squares and B pieces to make two flying-geese units (see page 75) measuring 1½" × 2½".

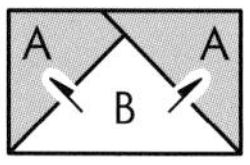

Make 2 units, 1½" × 2½".

2. Use B and C pieces to make two elongated flying-geese units (see page 76) measuring 1½" × 4½".

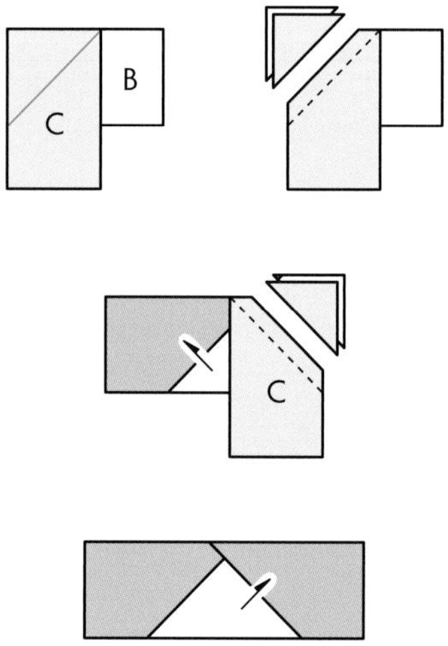

Make 2 units, 1½" × 4½".

3. Use D and E squares to make one square-in-a-square unit (see page 76) measuring 2½" square.

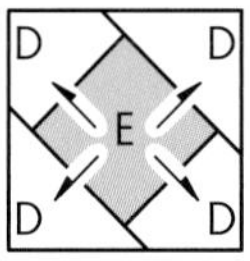

Make 1 unit,
2½" × 2½".

4. Arrange the units from steps 1–3 as shown. Join the units in the center row and then join the rows to make a block. Make one block measuring 4½" square.

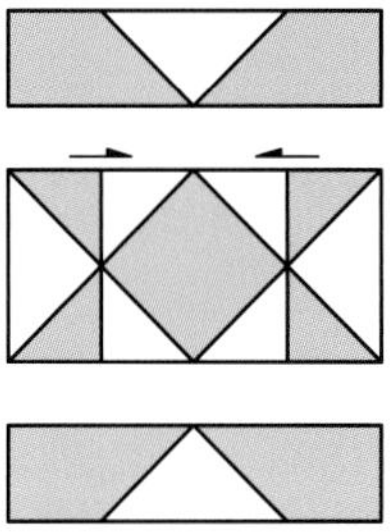

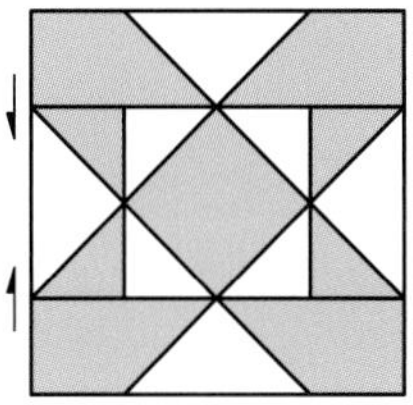

Make 1 block,
4½" × 4½".

BLOCK 20

CRISSCROSS

FINISHED BLOCK: 4" × 4"

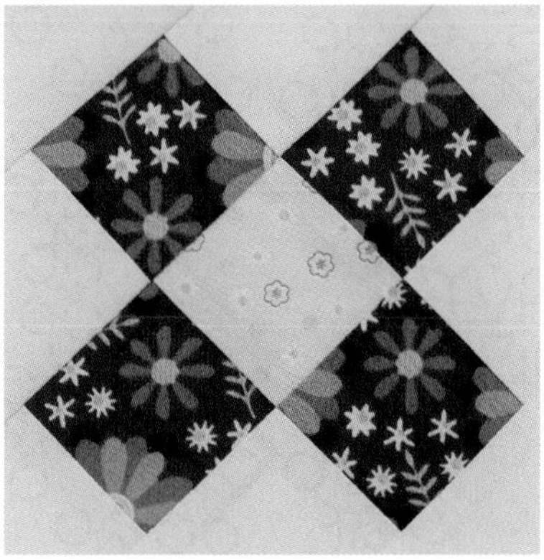

Materials

Materials are for making 4 blocks needed for the Barn Star Sampler. If you are making a different quilt, refer to the materials list for that project. I used fabrics 7, 8, and 25 for cross sections, fabrics 3, 4, and 8 for center squares, and fabrics 3 and 26 for backgrounds.

1 fat eighth *total* of assorted prints for cross sections (fabrics 7, 8, and 25)

1 fat eighth *total* of assorted prints for center squares (fabrics 4 and 8)

1 fat eighth of white print #2 for background (fabric 26)

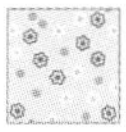
1 piece, 5" × 10", of coral floral for center square and background (fabric 3)

Cutting for 1 Block

The instructions yield pieces to make 1 block. Check instructions for the project you're making to see how many blocks are needed. Label pieces as you cut. The assembly diagrams refer to each piece by the letter that follows the dimensions.

From 1 of the prints for cross sections, cut:
4 □ 1⅞" × 1⅞" (A)

From 1 of the prints for center squares, cut:
1 □ 1⅞" × 1⅞" (B)

From 1 of the prints for background, cut:
1 ⊠ 3½" × 3½" (C)
2 ⧄ 2" × 2" (D)

Assembling Block 20

Lay out pieces A–D as shown. Sew the pieces into diagonal rows; join the rows. Press seam allowances as indicated by the arrows. Trim to 4½" square. Make one block.

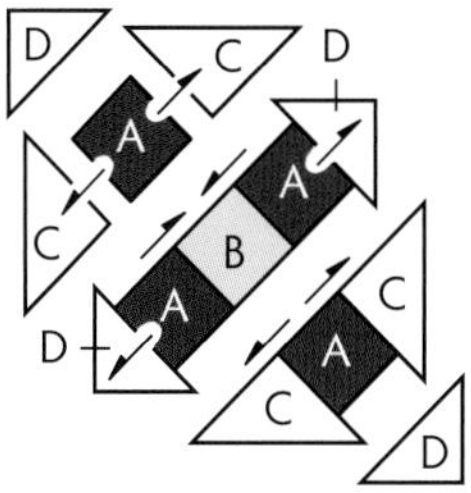

Make 1 block,
4½" × 4½".

Pieced by Shelley Cavanna; quilted by Cara Cansler.

COMPLETING THE BARN STAR SAMPLER

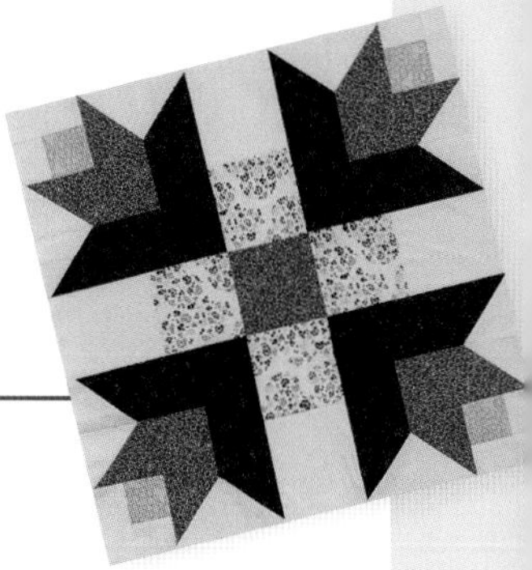

Additional Materials to Complete the Quilt

Yardage is based on 42"-wide fabric unless otherwise indicated.

⅞ yard of indigo print for binding (fabric 22)

7½ yards of fabric *OR* 2½ yards of 110"-wide fabric for backing

89" × 109" piece of batting

Cutting

From the indigo print, cut:
10 strips, 2½" × 42"

Making the Blocks

Referring to the individual block instructions (pages 12–37), cut and piece the following number of each block:

- Blocks 1–3: Make two of each block (24½" × 24½")
- Blocks 4–9: Make two of each block (16½" × 16½")
- Blocks 10–15: Make three of each block (8½" × 8½")
- Blocks 16–20: Make four of each block (4½" × 4½")

Assembling the Quilt Top

Because the blocks are not all the same size, it's impossible to simply sew the blocks together in rows and then join the rows. Instead, you'll be assembling the blocks in sections of various sizes, and then you'll join the sections. Press all seam allowances open.

Tips for Assembling Different-Sized Blocks

The best part of making a sampler quilt is *finally* assembling all the beautiful blocks. Here are a few tips to set yourself up for success:

- As you sew your blocks together, some of the seam allowances will nest and some won't. Both are fine!
- Do your best to match points and block edges when possible.
- If you have a stiletto or tailor's awl, this is a great time to use it. It can help you carefully and precisely feed your blocks through your sewing machine.
- Sometimes a seam intersection will fold over on itself as you're sewing. After piecing the block or row, take the time to go back and fix these areas so you don't have a bump along your seam.
- When fixing seams, don't rip out the whole block or row. Use your seam ripper to pop open a few seams on either side of the problem area, then re-pin and re-sew that area.
- You'll find that some seams will naturally want to fall open, while others will have a strong inclination to lean left or right. Just listen to your quilt top and press seams open *or* to one side!

SECTION A

1. Join one each of blocks 10 and 11. Sew one block 5 to the top to make a unit measuring 16½" × 24½".

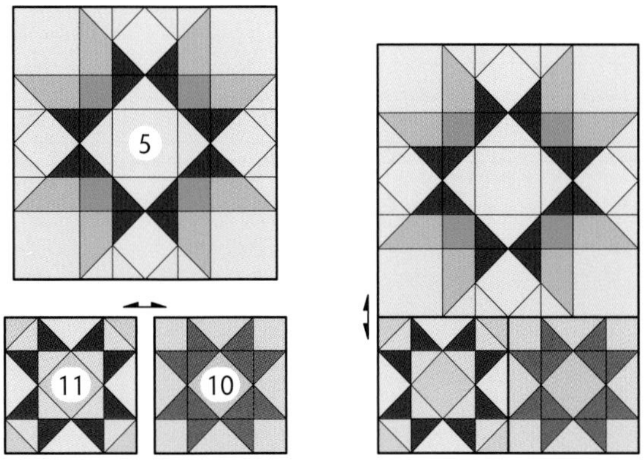

Make 1 unit,
16½" × 24½".

2. Join one each of blocks 12 and 13. Sew one block 9 to the bottom to make a unit measuring 16½" × 24½".

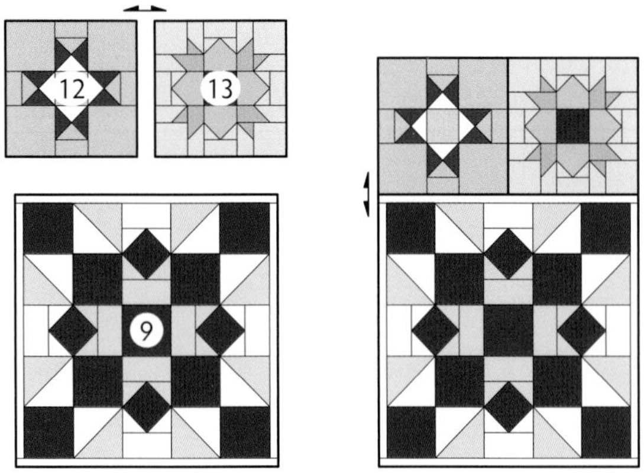

Make 1 unit,
16½" × 24½".

3. Join the units from steps 1 and 2 and one each of blocks 1 and 2 to make section A, which should measure 24½" × 80½".

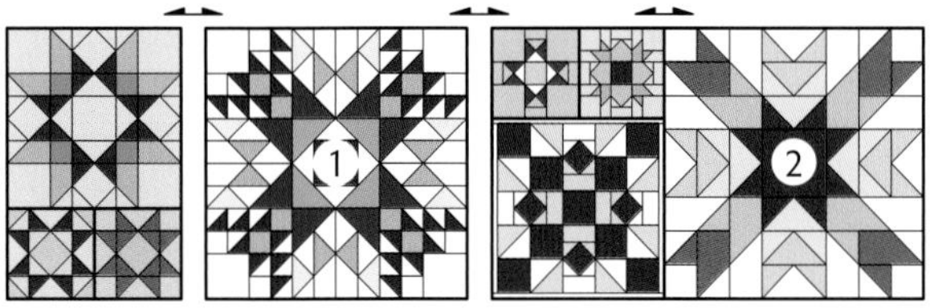

Make 1 A section,
24½" × 80½".

SECTION B

1. Join three each of blocks 16 and 20. Sew one block 3 to the bottom to make a unit measuring 24½" × 28½".

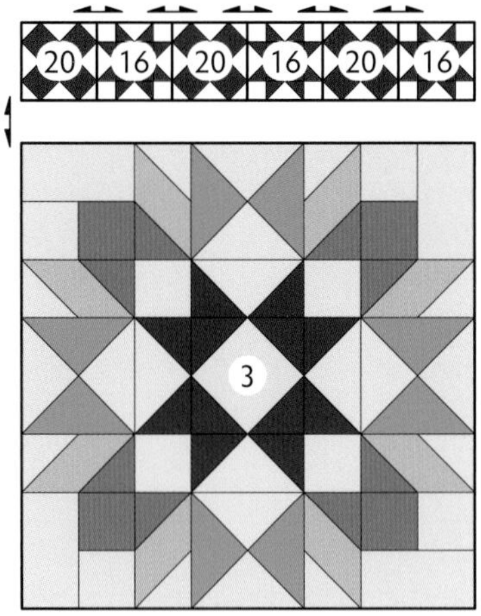

Make 1 unit,
24½" × 28½".

2. Arrange one each of blocks 4, 11, and 13, and four of block 19 as shown. Sew the blocks into rows and then join the rows to make a unit measuring 16½" × 28½".

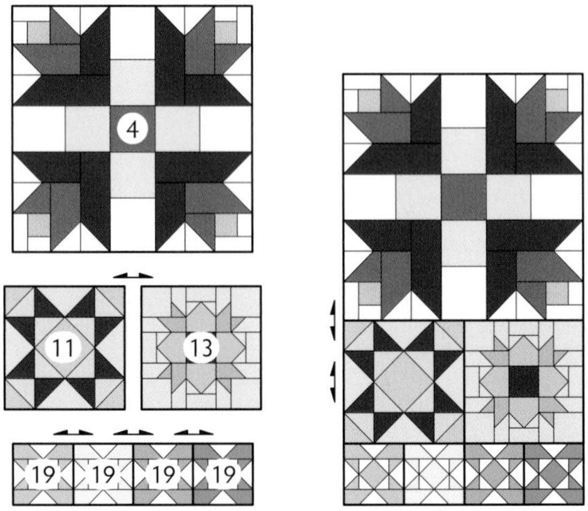

Make 1 unit,
16½" × 28½".

3. Join one each of blocks 16 and 20. Sew one block 15 to the top to make a unit measuring 8½" × 12½".

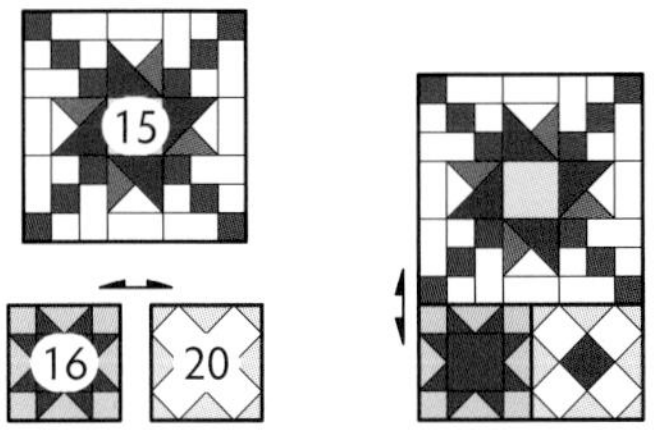

Make 1 unit,
8½" × 12½".

4. Join two of block 18. Sew one block 14 to the bottom to make a unit measuring 8½" × 12½".

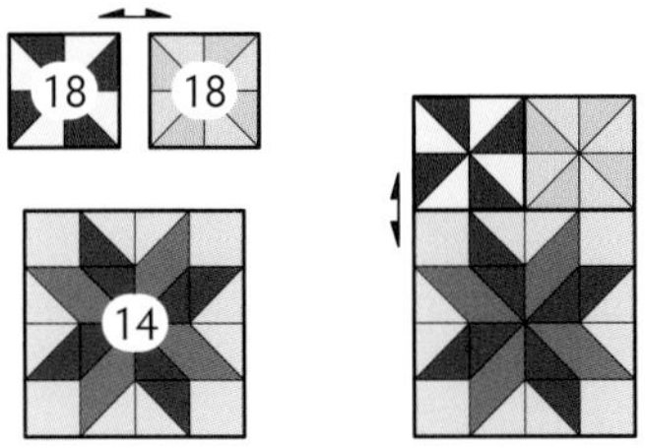

Make 1 unit,
8½" × 12½".

5. Join the units from steps 3 and 4. Sew one block 8 to the bottom to make a unit measuring 16½" × 28½".

Make 1 unit,
16½" × 28½".

6. Join the units from steps 1, 2, and 5 to make section B, which should measure 28½" × 56½".

Make 1 B section,
28½" × 56½".

SECTION C

1. Join one each of blocks 14 and 15. Sew one block 7 to the bottom and then add one block 2 to make a unit measuring 40½" × 24½".

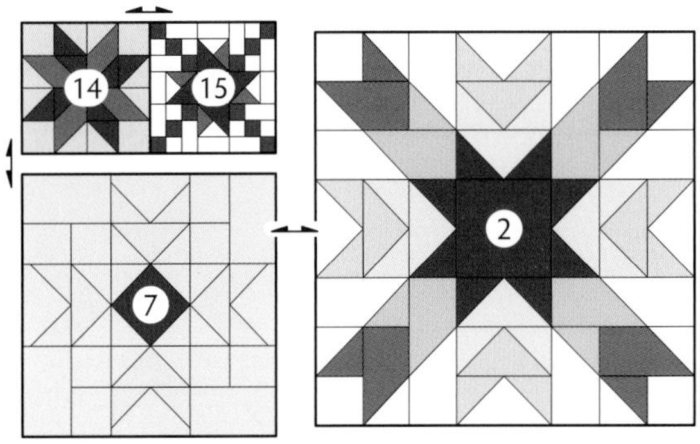

Make 1 unit,
40½" × 24½".

2. Join one each of blocks 11 and 14. Sew one block 6 to the bottom and then add one block 1 to make a unit measuring 40½" × 24½".

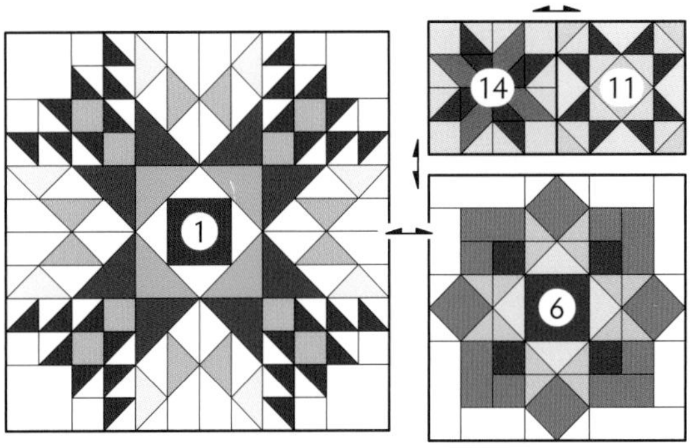

Make 1 unit,
40½" × 24½".

3. Join the units from steps 1 and 2. Join one each of blocks 4, 5, and 6 to make a column. Sew the column to the left side to make section C, which should measure 56½" × 48½".

Make 1 C section,
56½" × 48½".

SECTION D

1. Join blocks 12 and 13 and then add block 7 to make the top row. Join blocks 10 and 12 and then add block 9 to make the bottom row. Join the rows to make a unit measuring 24½" × 32½".

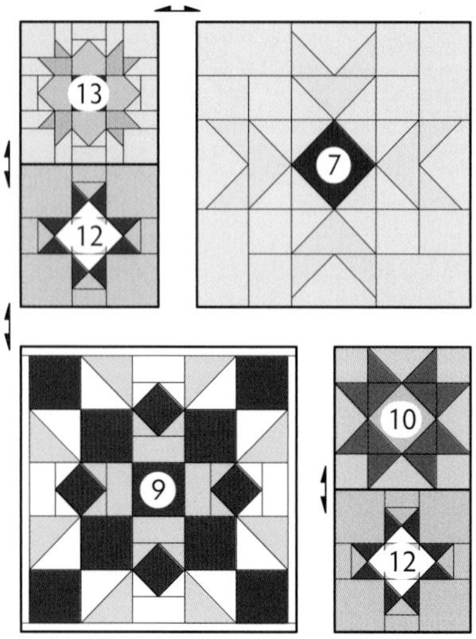

Make 1 unit,
24½" × 32½".

2. Join blocks 15 and 10. Sew block 8 to the right side to make the top row. Join four of block 17 and two of block 18 to make the center row. Join the rows and then add one block 3 to the bottom to make a unit measuring 24½" × 44½".

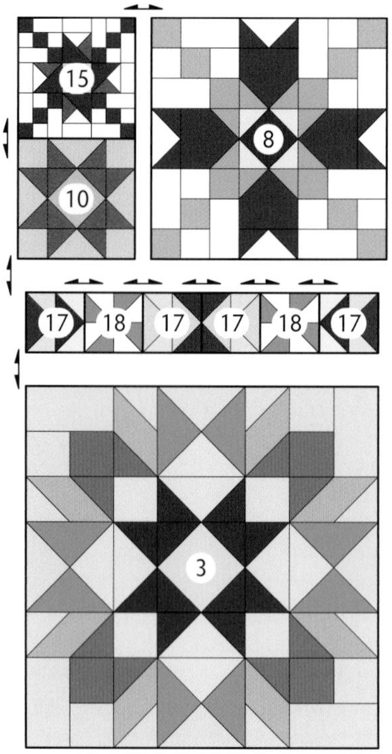

Make 1 unit,
24½" × 44½".

3. Join the units from steps 1 and 2 to make section D, which should measure 24½" × 76½".

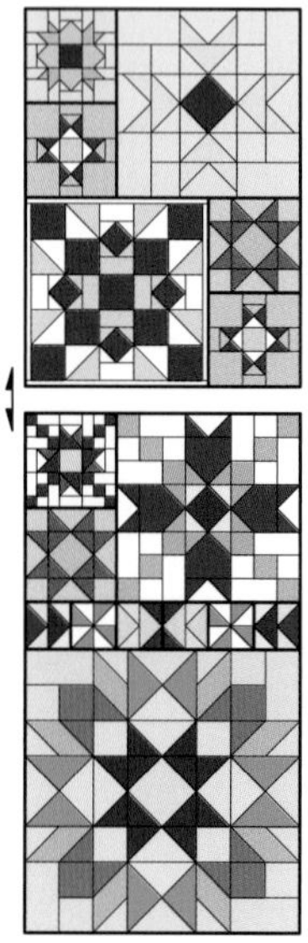

Make 1 D section,
24½" × 76½".

JOINING THE SECTIONS

Join sections B and C and then sew section D to the right edge. Sew section A to the top edge. The quilt top should measure 80½" × 100½".

Finishing the Quilt

1. Layer the quilt top, batting, and backing. Baste the layers together.

2. Hand or machine quilt. The quilt shown is machine quilted with an allover floral design.

3. Use the indigo 2½"-wide strips to make double-fold binding. Attach the binding to the quilt.

Quilt assembly

FLOWER FARM

Sweet and simple, the Flower Farm quilt was inspired by sunny spring afternoons spent wandering the aisles of my favorite local flower farm. It remixes the three units used in Block 1: Diamond Star for a fun and graphic mini-quilt.

FINISHED QUILT: 40½" × 40½"

FINISHED BLOCK: 8" × 8"

BLOCK USED: 1

Materials

Yardage is based on 42"-wide fabric. Fat quarters measure 18" × 21".

 1⅝ yards of white print #1 for background (fabric 25)

 ⅞ yard of dark indigo print for side and center units and binding (fabric 23)

 ⅜ yard of green print #1 for corner and side units (fabric 12)

 1 fat quarter of aqua floral #2 for side units (fabric 15)

 ½ yard of indigo floral for side units (fabric 21)

 1 fat quarter of medium aqua print for center units (fabric 18)

2½ yards of fabric for backing

45" × 45" piece of batting

Cutting

All measurements include ¼"-wide seam allowances. Label your pieces as you cut. The assembly diagrams refer to each piece by the letter that follows the dimensions.

From white print #1, cut:

32 □ 3" × 3" (A)
40 □ 2½" × 2½" (C)
8 □ 4½" × 4½" (E)
48 ▭ 2½" × 4½" (G)
24 ▭ 2½" × 6½" (H)
5 ⊠ 5½" × 5½" (L)

From the dark indigo print, cut:

32 □ 3" × 3" (B)
5 □ 4½" × 4½" (K)
5 strips, 2½" × 42"

From green print #1, cut:

16 □ 2½" × 2½" (D)
24 ▭ 2½" × 4½" (F)

Continued on page 46

Pieced by Shelley Cavanna; quilted by Cara Cansler.

Continued from page 45

From aqua floral #2, cut:
24 ▭ 2½" × 4½" (I)

From the indigo floral, cut:
24 □ 4½" × 4½" (J)

From the medium aqua print, cut:
10 ⊠ 5" × 5" (M)

Making the Blocks

Measurements for assembled pieces include seam allowances. Press seam allowances in the directions indicated by the arrows.

1. Follow instructions for "Making the Corner Units" on page 13. Use the A, B, C, D, and E pieces to make eight corner blocks measuring 8½" square.

2. Follow instructions for "Making the Side Units" on page 13. Use the C, F, G, H, I, and J pieces to make 12 side blocks measuring 8½" square.

3. Follow instructions for "Making the Center Units" on page 14. Use the K, L, and M pieces to make five center blocks measuring 8½" square.

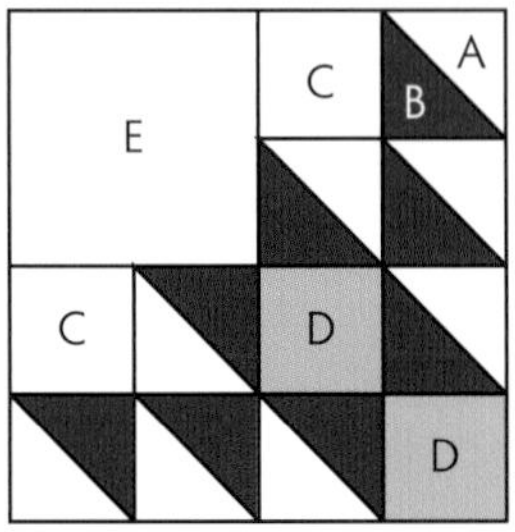

Make 8 corner blocks, 8½" × 8½".

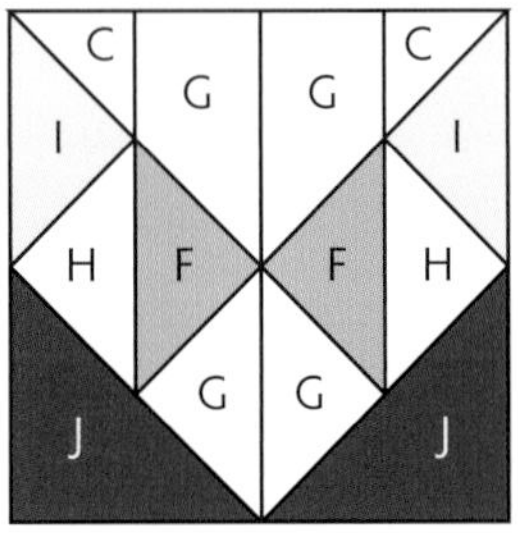

Make 12 side blocks, 8½" × 8½".

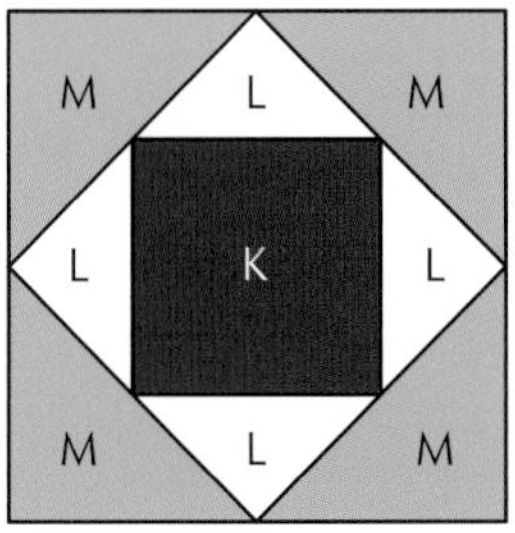

Make 5 center blocks, 8½" × 8½".

Assembling the Quilt Top

Arrange the corner, side, and center blocks in five rows, noting the orientation of each block. Sew the blocks into rows and then join the rows. The quilt top should measure 40½" square.

Quilt assembly

Finishing the Quilt

1. Layer the quilt top, batting, and backing. Baste the layers together.

2. Hand or machine quilt. The quilt shown is machine quilted with an allover floral and vine design.

3. Use the dark indigo 2½"-wide strips to make double-fold binding. Attach the binding to the quilt.

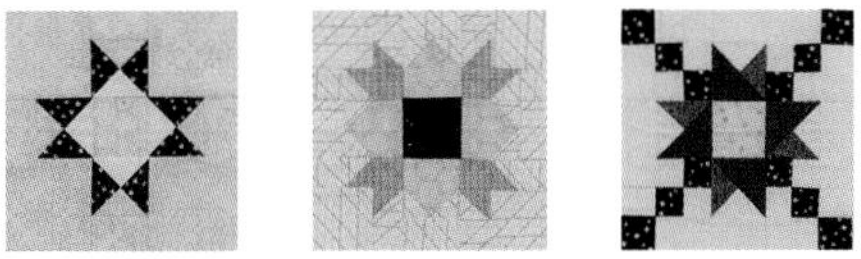

TEA FOR TWO

Easily create the illusion that the block patterns continue invisibly beyond the borders of the quilt by using the background fabric from block 13 for the setting triangles and the background fabric from block 12 for the corner triangles.

FINISHED QUILT: 47" × 47"

FINISHED BLOCK: 8" × 8"

BLOCKS USED: 12, 13, and 15

Materials

Yardage is based on 42"-wide fabric. Fat quarters measure 18" × 21". Fat eighths measure 9" × 21".

- ½ yard of white print #1 for blocks 12 and 15 (fabric 25)
- 1 square, 10" × 10", of light gold floral for block 12 (fabric 10)
- ⅝ yard of indigo floral for blocks 12 and 15, and border (fabric 21)
- ½ yard of coral print for block 12 and corner triangles (fabric 4)
- 1 fat eighth of aqua print for block 13 (fabric 17)
- 1 fat quarter of dark indigo print for block 13 and cornerstones (fabric 23)
- ½ yard of green print #2 for block 13 and binding (fabric 13)
- ¾ yard of light gray print #1 for block 13 and setting triangles (fabric 27)
- 1 square, 10" × 10", of coral floral for block 15 (fabric 3)
- 1 fat eighth of raspberry floral for block 15 (fabric 5)
- 1 fat eighth of dark raspberry print for block 15 (fabric 8)
- ¾ yard of light gray print #2 for sashing (fabric 28)

3 yards of fabric for backing

53" × 53" piece of batting

Cutting

All measurements include ¼" seam allowances. Label your pieces as you cut. The assembly diagrams refer to each piece by the letter that follows the dimensions.

To stay organized, I also label my pieces with the block number where they'll be used. For example, the A squares that will be used in block 12 are marked 12A.

CUTTING FOR BLOCK 12

Referring to "Block 12: Ohio Star" on page 29, follow the cutting instructions to cut pieces for four identical blocks.

CUTTING FOR BLOCK 13

Referring to "Block 13: Weathervane Star" on page 30, follow the cutting instructions to cut pieces for four identical blocks.

CUTTING FOR BLOCK 15

Referring to "Block 15: Windmill Star" on page 33, following the cutting instructions to cut pieces for five identical blocks.

ADDITIONAL CUTTING TO COMPLETE THE QUILT

From light gray print #2, cut:
36 ▭ 2½" × 8½"

From the dark indigo print, cut:
24 □ 2½" × 2½"

From the coral print, cut:
2 ◪ 6¾" × 6¾"

From light gray print #1, cut:
2 ⊠ 12¾" × 12¾"

From the indigo floral, cut:
5 strips, 2½" × 42"

From green print #2, cut:
5 strips, 2½" × 42"

Making the Blocks

Measurements listed for assembled pieces include seam allowances. Press seam allowances in the directions indicated by the arrows.

1. Using the pieces cut for block 12 and following the instructions on page 30, make four Ohio Star blocks measuring 8½" square.

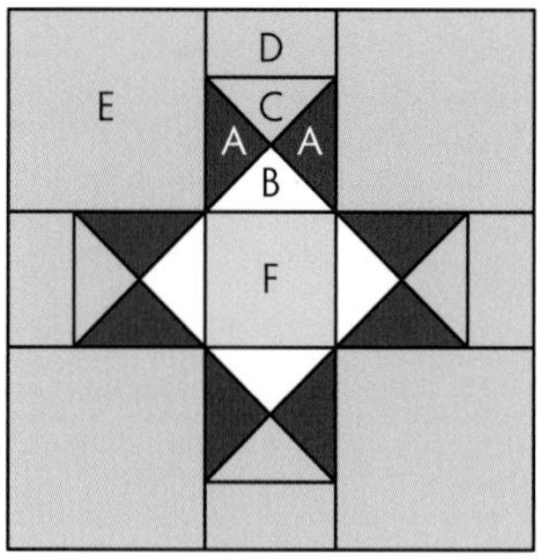

Block 12.
Make 4 blocks,
8½" × 8½".

2. Using the pieces cut for block 13 and following the instructions on page 31, make four Weathervane Star blocks measuring 8½" square.

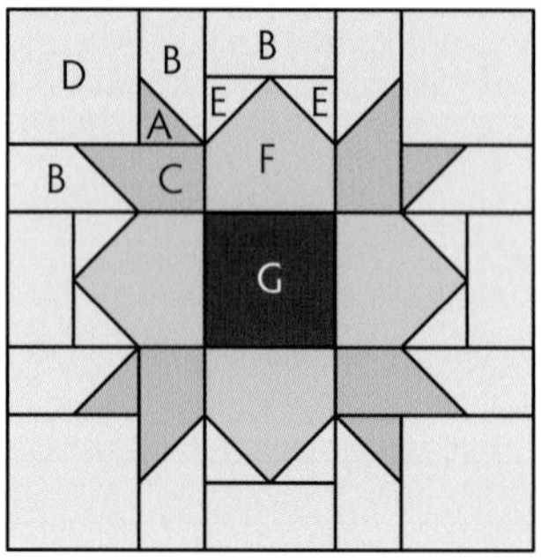

Block 13.
Make 4 blocks,
8½" × 8½".

Pieced by Shelley Cavanna; quilted by Cara Cansler.

3. Using the pieces cut for block 15 and following the instructions on page 33, make five Windmill Star blocks measuring 8½" square.

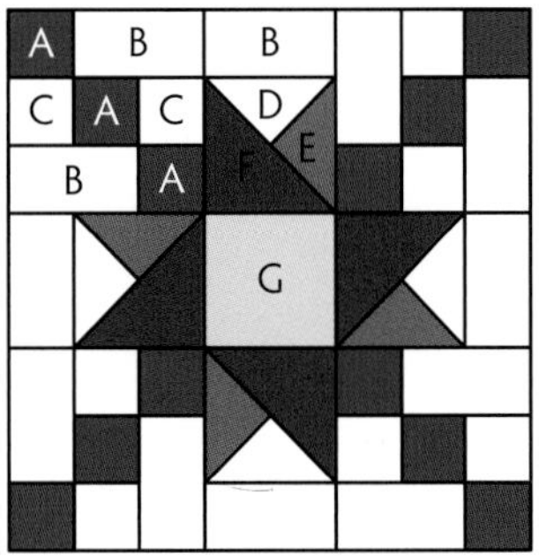

Block 15.
Make 5 blocks,
8½" × 8½".

Assembling the Quilt Top

1. Referring to the quilt assembly diagram, lay out the blocks, light gray strips, dark indigo 2½" squares, light gray triangles, and coral triangles in diagonal rows as shown. Join the gray strips and indigo squares to make sashing rows. Sew the blocks and gray strips into rows and then add the side triangles to make block rows. Join the rows, adding the corner triangles last.

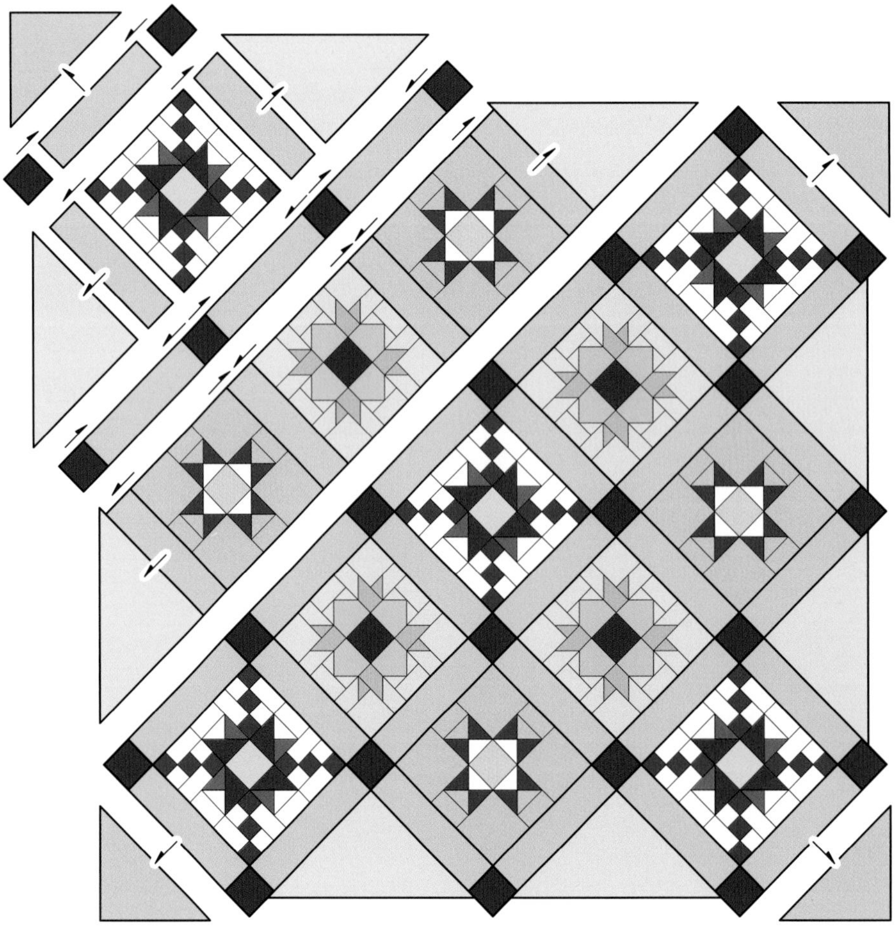

Quilt assembly

2. Trim and square up the quilt top, making sure to leave ¼" beyond the points of all gray strips for seam allowances. The quilt-top center should measure 43" square.

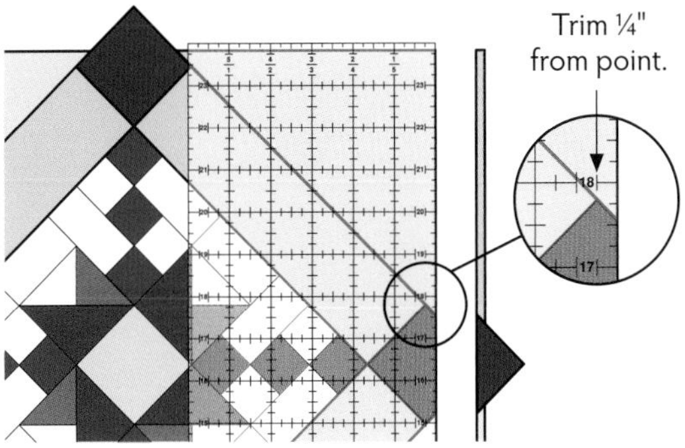

3. Join the indigo floral 2½"-wide strips end to end. From the pieced strip, cut two 47"-long strips and two 43"-long strips. Sew the shorter strips to the left and right sides of the quilt top. Sew the longer strips to the top and bottom edges. Press all seam allowances toward the border. The quilt top should measure 47" square.

Finishing the Quilt

1. Layer the quilt top, batting, and backing. Baste the layers together.

2. Hand or machine quilt. The quilt shown is machine quilted with an allover floral and vine design.

3. Use the green 2½"-wide strips to make double-fold binding. Attach the binding to the quilt.

CORDELIA

The first quilt I remember seeing is the one that lived on Anne's bed in her tiny attic bedroom under the eaves at Green Gables. Blocks 8 and 9 don't have a great deal in common on the surface, but just like Anne and Diana, when they come together, they create a beautiful friendship!

FINISHED QUILT: 64½" × 64½"

FINISHED BLOCK: 16" × 16"

BLOCKS USED: 8 and 9

Materials

Yardage is based on 42"-wide fabric. Fat quarters measure 18" × 21". The quilt shown uses the same white solid for the background in both blocks 8 and 9, which helps showcase the Irish chain motif created by combining the blocks.

⅜ yard of green print #1 for block 8 (fabric 12)

2¾ yards of white solid for blocks 8 and 9 background (fabric 24)

⅝ yard of medium aqua print for block 8 (fabric 18)

1⅛ yards of indigo floral for block 8 (fabric 21)

1 fat quarter of aqua floral #2 for block 8 (fabric 15)

⅞ yard of dark indigo print for block 8 and binding (fabric 23)

½ yard of coral floral for block 9 (fabric 3)

¾ yard of dark raspberry print for block 9 (fabric 7)

⅝ yard of plum floral for block 9 (fabric 9)

½ yard of white-and-raspberry print for block 9 (fabric 1)

4 yards of fabric for backing

71" × 71" piece of batting

Cutting

All measurements include ¼" seam allowances. Label your pieces as you cut. The assembly diagrams refer to each piece by the letter that follows the dimension. To stay organized, I also label my pieces with the block number where they'll be used. For example, the A squares that will be used in block 8 are marked 8A.

CUTTING FOR BLOCK 8

From green print #1, cut:
64 □ 2½" × 2½" (8A)

From the white solid, cut:
104 ▭ 2½" × 4½" (8B)
64 □ 2½" × 2½" (8C)

From the medium aqua print, cut:
112 □ 2½" × 2½" (8D)

From the indigo floral, cut:
40 □ 4½" × 4½" (8E)
80 □ 2½" × 2½" (8F)

From aqua floral #2, cut:
48 □ 2½" × 2½" (8G)

From the dark indigo print, cut:
12 □ 4½" × 4½" (8H)

CUTTING FOR BLOCK 9

From the white solid, cut:
32 □ 4" × 4" (9A)
80 □ 2" × 2" (9F)
40 ▭ 2" × 3½" (9H)
10 strips, 1" × 15½" (9I)
14 strips, 1" × 16½" (9J)
12 strips, 1" × 9½"
4 strips, 1" × 10"

From the coral floral, cut:
32 □ 4" × 4" (9B)

From the dark raspberry print, cut:
72 □ 3½" × 3½" (9C)

From the plum floral, cut:
45 □ 3½" × 3½" (9D)

From the white-and-raspberry print, cut:
40 ▭ 2" × 3½" (9G)
80 □ 2" × 2" (9E)

CUTTING FOR BINDING

From the dark indigo print, cut:
7 strips, 2½" × 42"

Making Block 8

You will be making four full blocks and eight half bocks. Measurements listed for assembled pieces include seam allowances. Press seam allowances in the directions indicated by the arrows.

1. Using the pieces cut for block 8 and the instructions on page 25, make the following units:

- 32 corner units measuring 6½" square
- 40 side units measuring 4½" × 6½"
- 12 center units measuring 4½" square

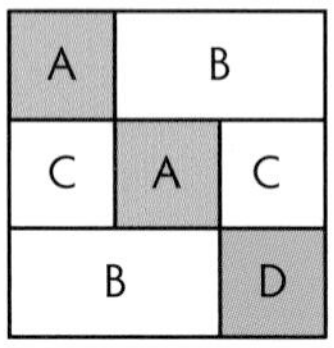

Make 32 corner units, 6½" × 6½".

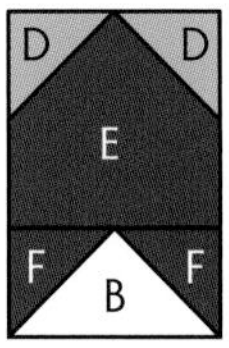

Make 40 side units, 4½" × 6½".

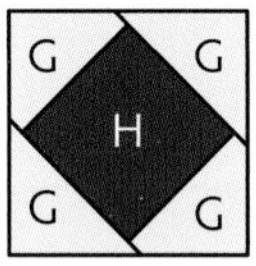

Make 12 center units, 4½" × 4½".

2. Arrange four corner units, four side units, and one center unit in three rows. Sew the units into rows and then join the rows. Make four blocks measuring 16½" square.

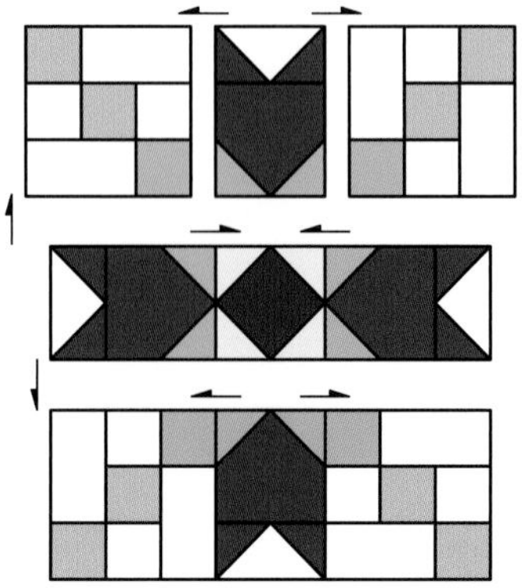

Block 8.
Make 4 blocks,16½" × 16½".

Pieced by Shelley Cavanna; quilted by Cara Cansler.

3. Arrange three side units, two corner units, and one center unit in two rows. Sew the units into rows and then join the rows. Make eight half blocks measuring 16½" × 10½".

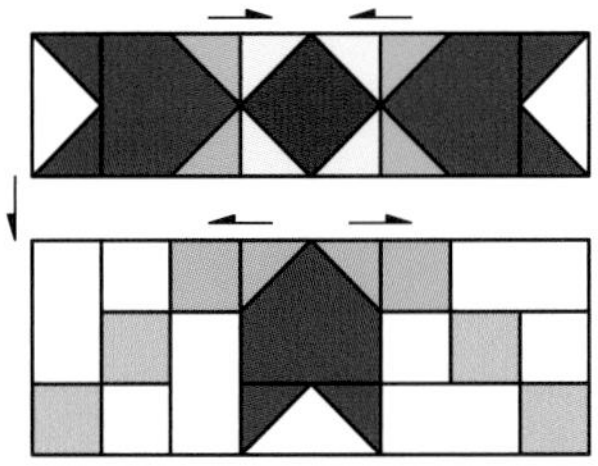

Make 8 half blocks, 16½" × 10½".

Making Block 9

You will be making five full blocks, four half blocks, and four quarter blocks. Measurements listed for assembled pieces include seam allowances. Press seam allowances in the directions indicated by the arrows.

1. Using the pieces cut for block 9 and the instructions on page 26, make the following units:

- 32 corner units measuring 6½" square
- 40 side units measuring 3½" × 6½"

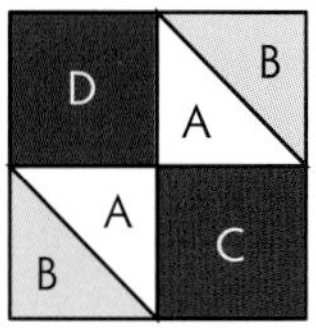

Make 32 corner units, 6½" × 6½".

Make 40 side units, 3½" × 6½".

2. Arrange four corner units, four side units, and one D square in three rows. Sew all the pieces into rows and then join the rows. Sew one I strip to the left and one I strip to the right side of the block. Sew J strips to the top and bottom edges. Make five blocks measuring 16½" square.

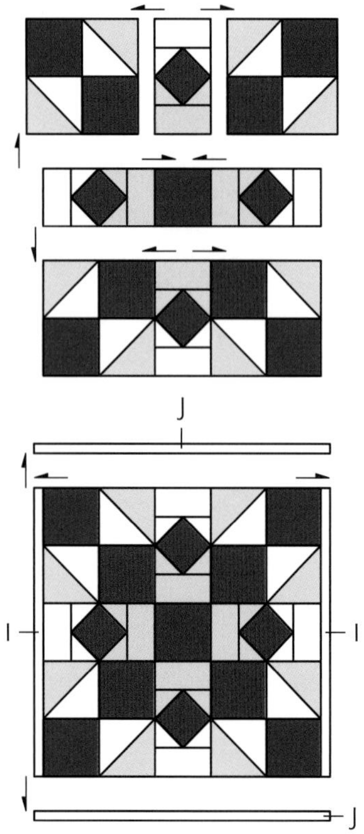

Block 9.
Make 5 blocks, 16½" × 16½".

3. Arrange three side units, two corner units, and one D square in two rows. Sew all the pieces into rows and then join the rows. Sew white 1" × 9½" strips to the left and right edges. Sew a J strip to the bottom edge. Make four half blocks measuring 16½" × 10".

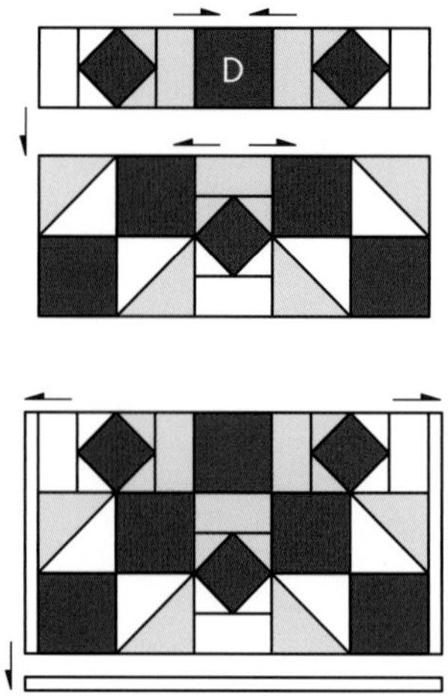

Make 4 half blocks, 16½" × 10".

4. Arrange two side units, one corner unit, and one D square in two rows. Sew all the pieces into rows and then join the rows. Sew a white 1" × 9½" strip to the right edge and then sew a white 1" × 10" strip to the bottom. Make four quarter blocks measuring 10" square.

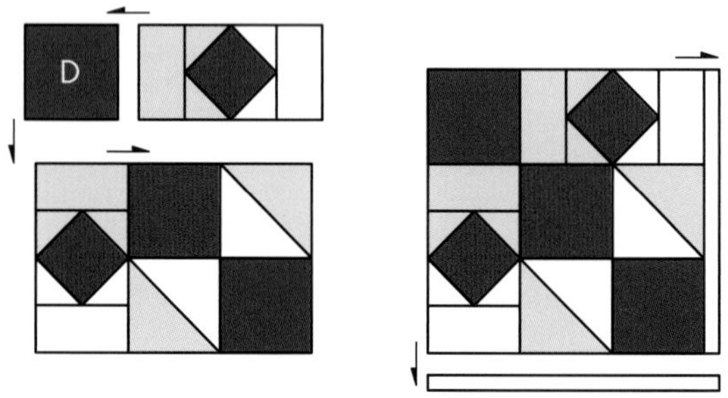

Make 4 quarter blocks, 10" × 10".

Assembling the Quilt Top

1. Referring to the quilt assembly diagram, lay out the blocks, half blocks, and quarter blocks in five rows. Sew the blocks into rows and then join the rows. You'll

notice that the edges of the half and quarter blocks won't line up around the perimeter. Don't worry, the edges will be trimmed in the next step.

Quilt assembly

2. Trim and square up the quilt top, making sure to leave ¼" beyond the points on all blocks for seam allowances. The quilt top should measure 64½" square.

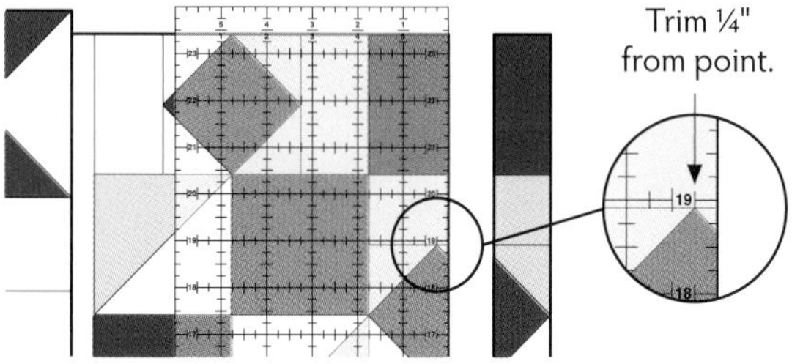

Finishing the Quilt

1. Layer the quilt top, batting, and backing. Baste the layers together.

2. Hand or machine quilt. The quilt shown is machine quilted with an allover diamond motif.

3. Use the dark indigo 2½"-wide strips to make double-fold binding. Attach the binding to the quilt.

MAP
UNITED STATES
TERRITORIES

LAKESIDE

One of my favorite summer destinations is the western shores of Lake Tahoe, California. This picnic-perfect quilt is terrific for spending an afternoon at the lake, snoozing in the sun or getting lost in a really good book.

FINISHED QUILT: 64½" × 80½"

FINISHED BLOCK: 16" × 16"

BLOCKS USED: 5 and 6

Materials

Yardage is based on 42"-wide fabric.

- 1½ yards of light gray print #1 for block 5 (fabric 27)
- ¾ yard of green print #2 for block 5 (fabric 13)
- ⅜ yard of teal print for block 5 (fabric 19)
- 2 yards of indigo print for blocks 5 and 6, and binding (fabric 22)
- 1¼ yards of aqua floral #1 for block 5 (fabric 14)
- 1⅜ yards of teal floral for block 6 (fabric 20)
- 1½ yards of white print #2 for block 6 (fabric 26)
- 1¼ yards of aqua print for blocks 5 and 6 (fabric 17)
- ½ yard of light gray print #2 for block 6 (fabric 28)

5 yards of fabric for backing

73" × 89" piece of batting

Cutting

All measurements include ¼" seam allowances. Label your pieces as you cut. The assembly diagrams refer to each piece by the letter that follows the dimensions. To stay organized, I also label my pieces with the block number where they'll be used. For example, the A squares that will be used in block 5 are marked 5A.

CUTTING FOR BLOCK 5

Referring to "Block 5: Northern Star" on page 21, follow the cutting instructions to cut pieces for 10 identical blocks.

CUTTING FOR BLOCK 6

Referring to "Block 6: Moroccan Star" on page 22, follow the cutting instructions to cut pieces for 10 identical blocks.

ADDITIONAL CUTTING TO COMPLETE THE QUILT

From the aqua print, cut:
80 ☐ 2½" × 2½"

From the indigo print, cut:
8 strips, 2½" × 42"

Making the Blocks

Measurements listed for assembled pieces include seam allowances. Press seam allowances in the directions indicated by the arrows.

1. Using the pieces cut for block 5 and the instructions on page 21, make 10 of block 5.

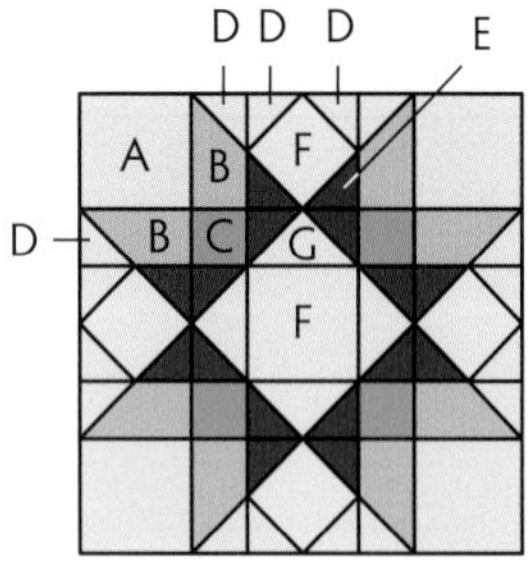

Block 5.

2. Sew aqua 2½" squares to the corners of each block (see page 74). Make 10 blocks measuring 16½" square.

Block 5.
Make 10 blocks,
16½" × 16½".

3. Using the pieces cut for block 6 and following the instructions on page 23, make 10 of block 6.

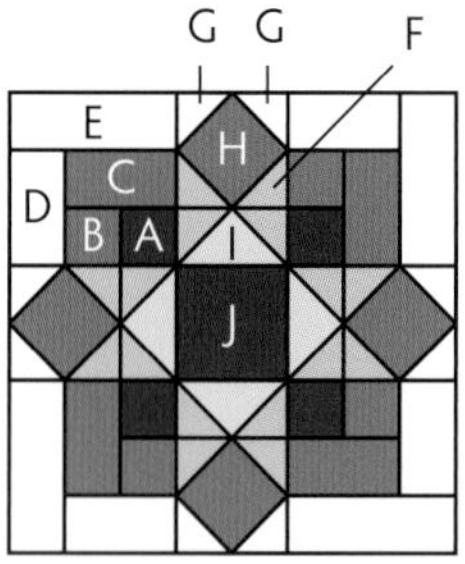

Block 6.

4. Sew aqua 2½" squares to the corners of each block. Make 10 blocks measuring 16½" square.

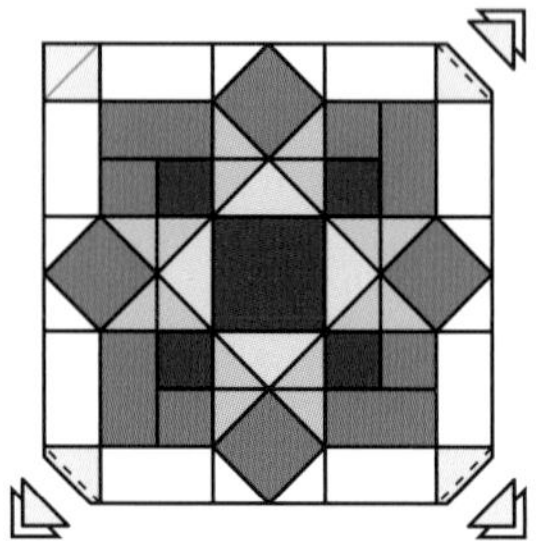

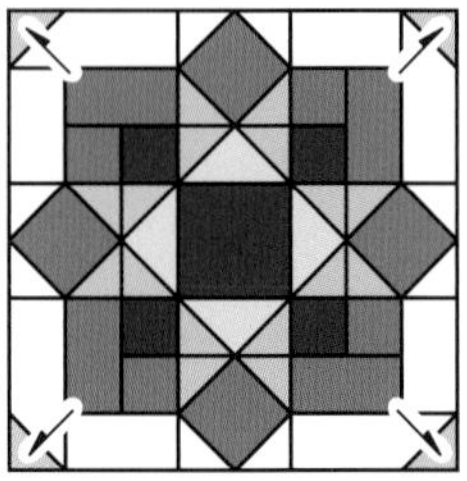

Block 6.
Make 10 blocks,
16½" × 16½".

> **TEST YOUR SEAM ALLOWANCES**
>
> Sewing with a ¼" presser foot doesn't guarantee accurate seams, so take the time to make sure that your ¼" seam is true. To test, cut two 2½" squares. Sew them together and press the seam allowances open. The unit should measure 2½" × 4½".

Pieced by Shelley Cavanna; quilted by Cara Cansler.

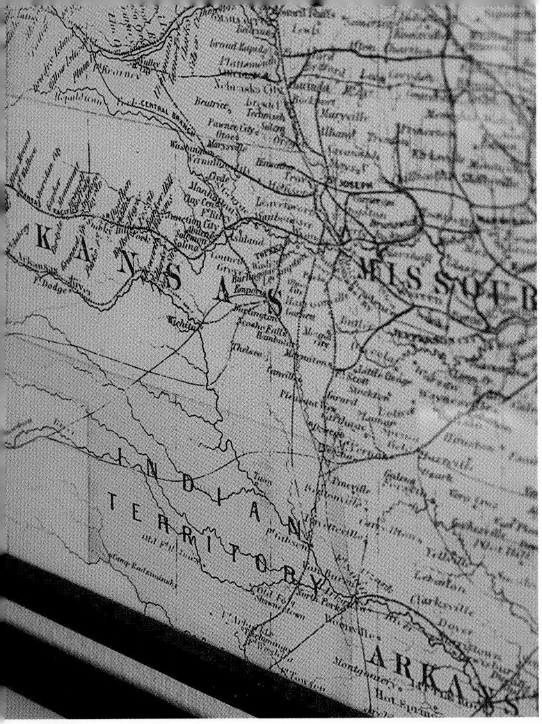

Assembling the Quilt Top

Referring to the quilt assembly diagram, lay out the blocks in five rows of four blocks each, alternating their positions in each row. Sew the blocks into rows and then join the rows. The quilt top should measure 64½" × 80½".

Quilt assembly

Finishing the Quilt

1. Layer the quilt top, batting, and backing. Baste the layers together.

2. Hand or machine quilt. The quilt shown is machine quilted with an allover looping swirl design.

3. Use the indigo 2½"-wide strips to make double-fold binding. Attach the binding to the quilt.

PRAIRIE ROSE

While the original Carpenter Star block from the Barn Star Sampler (page 11) uses some of my very favorite blue, teal, and aqua prints, I just couldn't resist making an alternate version featuring some pretty, dainty prints in various shades of plum, cherry, and coral! I love how the simple addition of stitch-and-flip corners and a few flying-geese units in the borders create such a fun and interesting secondary floral pattern.

FINISHED QUILT: 78½" × 78½"

FINISHED BLOCK: 24" × 24"

BLOCK USED: 3

Materials

Yardage is based on 42"-wide fabric.

- 2¾ yards of white print #1 for background and border (fabric 25)
- 1⅛ yards of dark raspberry floral for blocks (fabric 7)
- 1⅜ yards of coral print for blocks (fabric 4)
- 1⅝ yards of white-and-raspberry print for blocks (fabric 1)
- 1⅝ yards of plum floral for blocks and binding (fabric 9)
- 1⅛ yards of dark raspberry print for blocks (fabric 8)
- 1⅜ yards of light gray print #2 for border (fabric 28)

7¼ yards of fabric for backing

87" × 87" square of batting

Cutting

All measurements include ¼" seam allowances. Label your pieces as you cut. The assembly diagrams refer to each piece by the letter that follows the dimensions.

From white print #1, cut:
108 □ 3½" × 3½" (A)
48 ▭ 3½" × 6½" (C)
9 □ 6½" × 6½" (K)
9 ⊠ 7½" × 7½" (F)

From the dark raspberry floral, cut:
108 □ 3½" × 3½" (B)

From the coral print, cut:
72 ▭ 3½" × 6½" (D)

From the white-and-raspberry print, cut:
36 □ 3½" × 3½" (E)
36 ▭ 3½" × 6½" (J)
9 ⊠ 7½" × 7½" (H)

From the plum floral, cut:
18 ⊠ 7½" × 7½" (G)
9 strips, 2½" × 42"

From the dark raspberry print, cut:
108 □ 3½" × 3½" (I)

From light gray print #2, cut:
64 □ 3½" × 3½" (L)
24 ▭ 3½" × 9½" (M)

Making the Blocks

Measurements listed for assembled pieces include seam allowances. Press seam allowances in the directions indicated by the arrows.

1. Using pieces A–K and following the instructions on page 17, make nine Carpenter Star blocks.

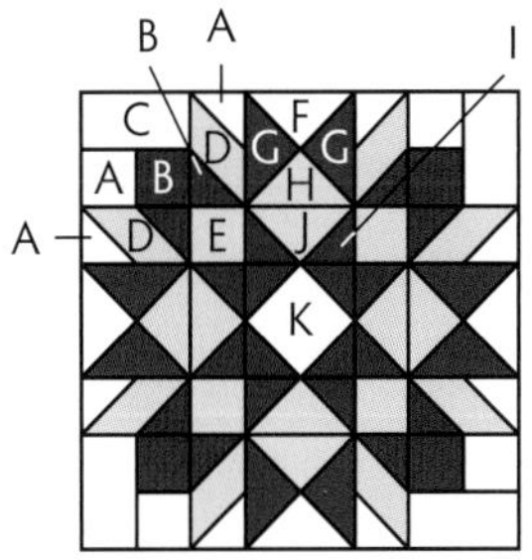

Block 3.

2. Sew L squares to the corners of each block (see page 74). Make nine blocks measuring 24½" square.

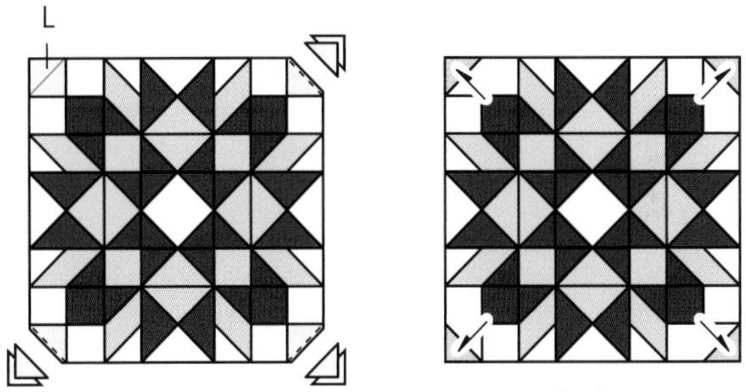

Block 3.
Make 9 blocks,
24½" × 24½".

Making the Border Units

1. Use L squares and C pieces to make 12 flying-geese units (see page 75) measuring 3½" × 6½".

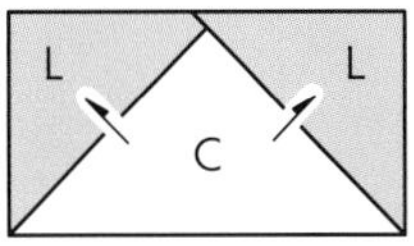

Make 12 units,
3½" × 6½".

2. Sew one M strip to each end of a flying-geese unit. Make 12 border units measuring 3½" × 24½".

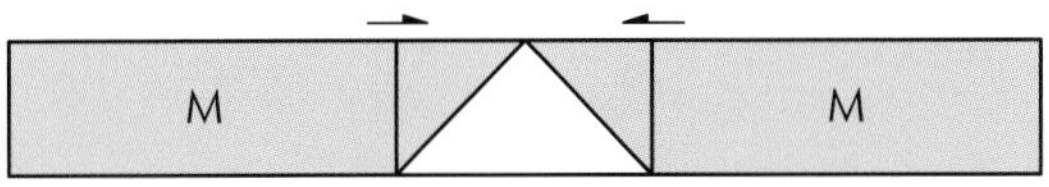

Make 12 units,
3½" × 24½".

Pieced by Shelley Cavanna; quilted by Cara Cansler.

Assembling the Quilt Top

Referring to the quilt assembly diagram, lay out the blocks, border units, and the four remaining L squares in five rows as shown. Sew all the pieces into rows and then join the rows. The quilt top should measure 78½" square.

Quilt assembly

Finishing the Quilt

1. Layer the quilt top, batting, and backing. Baste the layers together.

2. Hand or machine quilt. The quilt shown is machine quilted with an allover swirling floral design.

3. Use the plum floral 2½"-wide strips to make double-fold binding. Attach the binding to the quilt.

Nº9

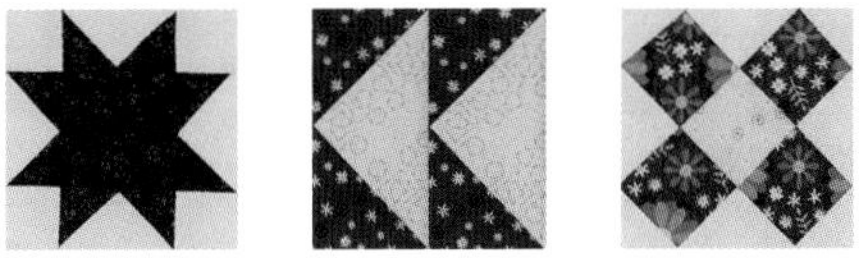

BAKING DAY

It might seem strange for the easiest project in the book to come at the end, but if you've worked your way through several of the previous projects then chances are you have a lovely little stack of triangle trimmings left over from piecing those larger blocks. Baking Day is a fantastic opportunity to repurpose some of those triangles into a sweet and scrappy table runner with a handmade, patchwork feel.

FINISHED RUNNER: 64½" × 16½"
FINISHED BLOCK: 4" × 4"
BLOCKS USED: 16, 17, and 20

Materials

All measurements include ¼" seam allowances.

1 yard *total* of assorted prints in coral, berry, plum, and green (collectively referred to as "dark") for blocks

1 yard *total* of assorted white and light prints for background

½ yard of plum floral for binding (fabric 9)

1⅜ yards of fabric for backing

23" × 71" piece of batting

Cutting

All measurements include ¼" seam allowances. Label your pieces as you cut. The assembly diagrams refer to each piece by the letter that follows the dimensions. To stay organized, I also label my pieces with the block number where they'll be used. For example, the A squares that will be used in block 16 are marked 16A.

CUTTING FOR BLOCK 16

Cutting is for 1 block. Repeat to cut 10 blocks from assorted fabrics.

From 1 dark print, cut:
8 □ 1½" × 1½" (16A)
1 □ 2½" × 2½" (16D)

From 1 white or light print, cut:
4 ▭ 1½" × 2½" (16B)
4 □ 1½" × 1½" (16C)

Continued on page 72

Continued from page 71

CUTTING FOR BLOCK 17

Cutting is for 1 block. Repeat to cut 44 blocks from assorted fabrics.

From *each* of 2 white or light prints, cut:
2 □ 2½" × 2½" (4 total, 17A)

From *each* of 2 dark prints, cut:
1 ▭ 2½" × 4½" (2 total, 17B)

CUTTING FOR BLOCK 20

Cutting is for 1 block. Repeat to cut 10 blocks.

From 1 dark print, cut:
4 □ 1⅞" × 1⅞" (20A)

From 1 dark print, cut:
1 □ 1⅞" × 1⅞" (20B)

From 1 white or light print, cut:
1 ⊠ 3½" × 3½" (20C)
2 ⧄ 2" × 2" (20D)

ADDITIONAL CUTTING TO COMPLETE THE TABLE RUNNER

From the plum floral, cut:
5 strips, 2½" × 42"

Scrap Economy

If you'd like to be even more economical with your scraps, you can sew together two half-square-triangle units to make a faux flying-geese unit. For my sample runner, I used assorted scraps from the projects in this book, along with a few prints from my stash that happened to match my color palette perfectly!

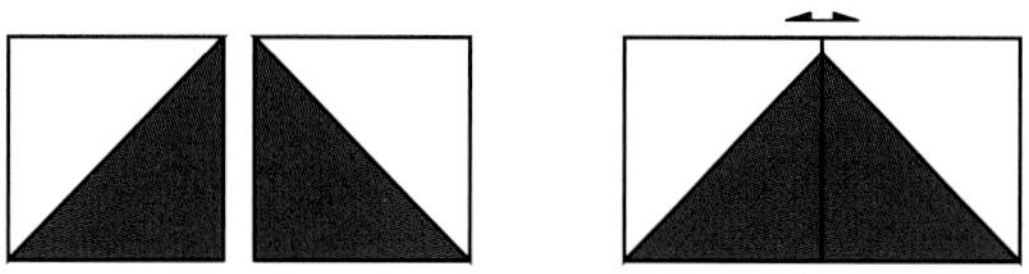

Making the Blocks

Measurements listed for assembled pieces include seam allowances. Press seam allowances in the directions indicated by the arrows.

1. Using the pieces cut for block 16 and the instructions on page 34, make 10 of block 16 measuring 4½" square.

2. Using the pieces cut for block 17 and the instructions on page 35, make 44 of block 17 measuring 4½" square.

3. Using the pieces cut for block 20 and the instructions page 37, make 10 of block 20 measuring 4½" square.

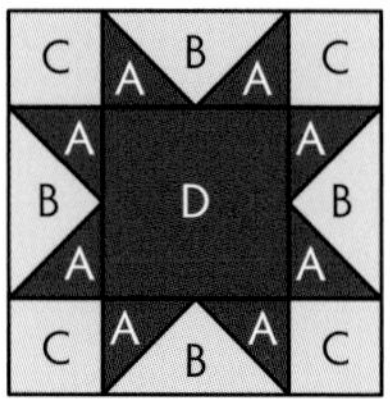

Block 16.
Make 10 blocks,
4½" × 4½".

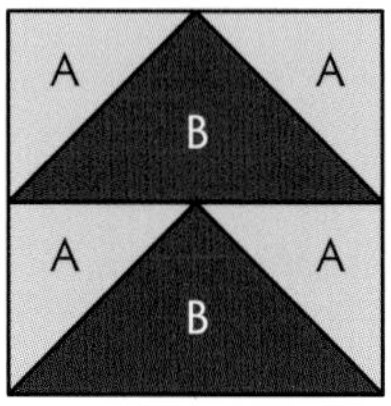

Block 17.
Make 44 blocks,
4½" × 4½".

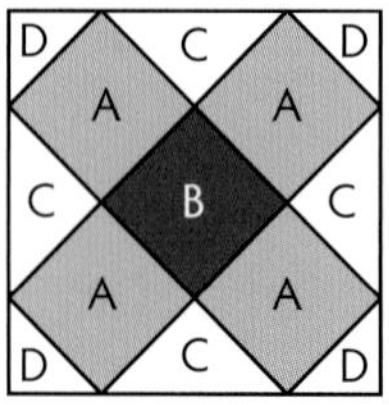

Block 20.
Make 10 blocks,
4½" × 4½".

Pieced by Shelley Cavanna; quilted by Cara Cansler.

Assembling the Table-Runner Top

Referring to the table-runner assembly diagram, lay out the blocks in four rows of 16 as shown. Sew the blocks into rows and then join the rows. The table runner should measure 64½" × 16½".

Finishing the Table Runner

1. Layer the runner top, batting, and backing. Baste the layers together.

2. Hand or machine quilt. The table runner shown is machine quilted with an allover swirling paisley design.

3. Use the plum floral 2½"-wide strips to make double-fold binding. Attach the binding to the runner.

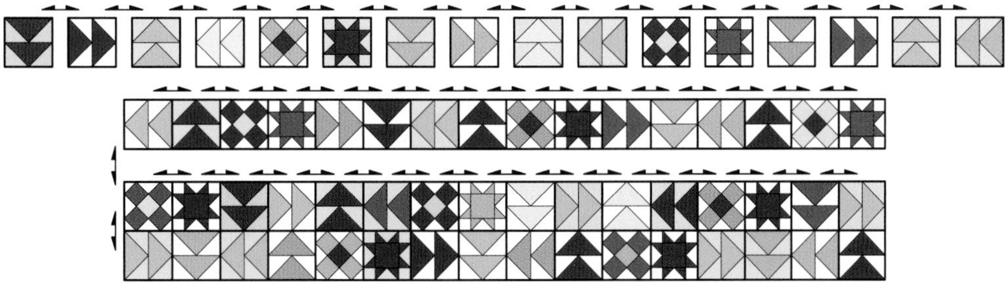

Table-runner assembly

SPECIAL TECHNIQUES

In this section, you'll find tutorials for some of the units or "building blocks" frequently used throughout the book. Refer to these tutorials as needed, but look to the instructions and illustrations in each project for the exact pieces to use and the angle or placement of the sewing lines.

In designing the blocks and quilts in this book, I've used my favorite stitch-and-flip techniques to eliminate as many of the triangles and bias edges as I could. I prefer this method of piecing because, in my experience, it's faster and yields the most accurate units with the least amount of fuss!

For blocks that do need triangles or use bias edges, you'll cut oversized pieces whenever possible. After sewing and pressing, the pieces will be trimmed to the exact size needed.

While none of the building blocks and shapes used to assemble the Barn Stars are particularly hard, they are complex, so you'll want to set yourself up for success by piecing as accurately as possible!

Stitch-and-Flip Units

The stitch-and-flip assembly method is a fantastic way to quickly and easily piece blocks that contain a 45° angled seam without sewing any bias edges or using templates or triangles. This method uses very few fabric pieces and usually just a seam or two.

CORNER UNIT

The most basic stitch-and-flip unit is a stitch-and-flip corner. It's a very simple and efficient way to embed a triangle in a quilt block.

Start by drawing a diagonal line from corner to corner on the wrong side of a square. This will be your stitching line. Pin the marked square to the base piece, right sides together. Sew on the marked line. Trim the excess corner fabric ¼" from the stitched line and press as directed.

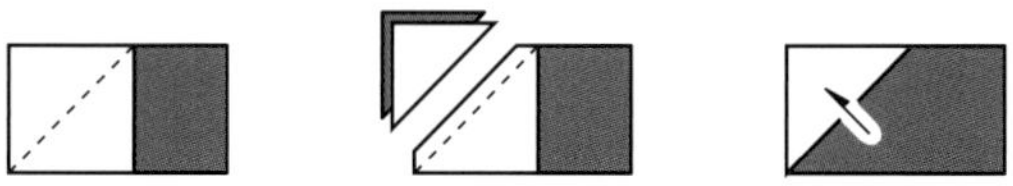

Corner unit

FLYING GEESE

Flying geese can easily be made by adding stitch-and-flip corners to the left and then right ends of a base piece.

Draw a diagonal line from corner to corner on the wrong side of a square. Pin the marked square to the base piece, right sides together. Sew on the marked line, then trim the excess corner fabric ¼" from the stitched line. Place a marked square on the opposite end of the base piece, making sure the marked line is oriented as shown. Sew and trim as before to make a flying-geese unit.

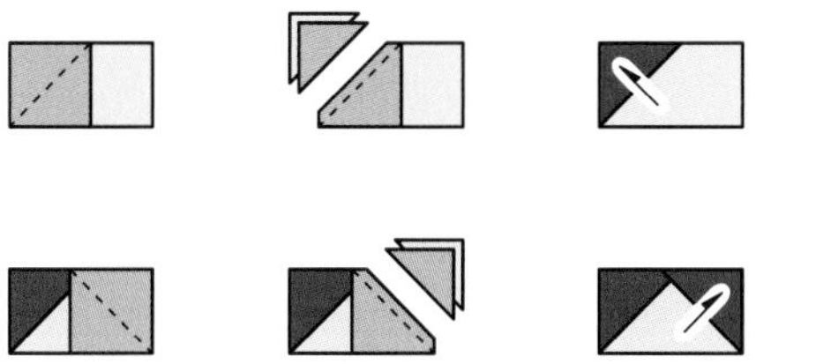

Flying-geese unit

HOUSE UNIT

Square or rectangular house units can be made using the same method as the flying geese. Just substitute a square or a larger piece as the base piece.

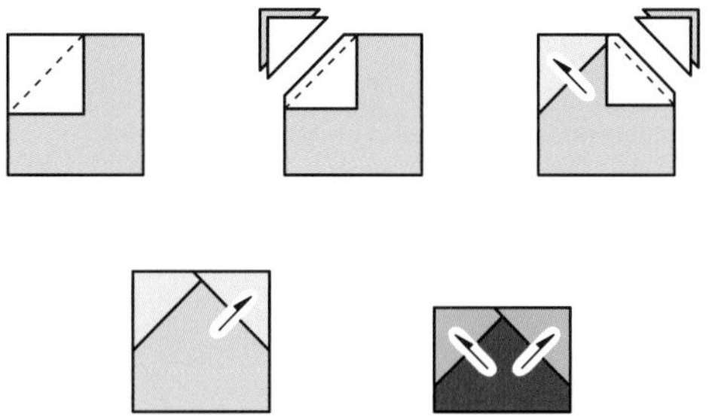

Square house unit   Rectangle house unit

> **Press for Success**
>
> Be gentle with your iron! Before pressing, open the unit with your fingertips and then press using an up-and-down motion with your iron. Try to avoid pushing the unit around with the iron so that you don't distort the seam.

SQUARE-IN-A-SQUARE UNIT

Make a square-in-a-square unit by adding a stitch-and-flip corner to all four corners of a base square.

Draw a diagonal line from corner to corner on the wrong side of four small squares. Place marked squares on opposite corners of a larger square. Sew on the marked lines. Trim the excess corner fabric ¼" from the stitched lines. Place marked squares on the remaining corners of the square; sew and trim as before.

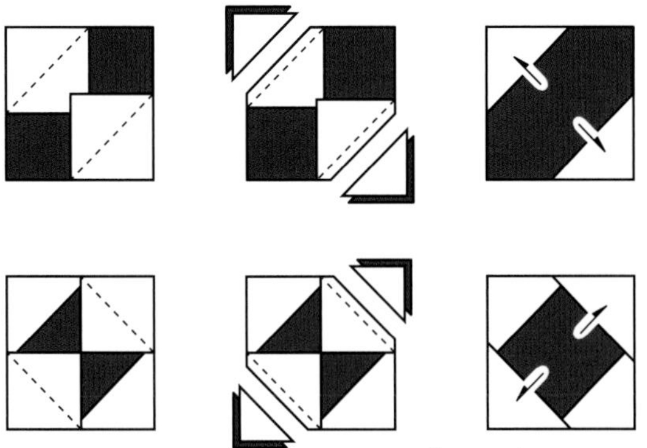

Square-in-a-square unit

This technique works best for units that are smaller than 4½" square. For larger square-in-a-square units, I use oversized triangles and trim the units to the correct size.

RECTANGULAR UNIT AND ELONGATED FLYING-GEESE UNIT

The stitch-and-flip technique can also be used to make leaning rectangular units and elongated flying-geese units.

To make a rectangular unit, pin a rectangle as instructed to a base rectangle, right sides together. Make sure that the corners are aligned and then mark the diagonal sewing line as shown. Sew on the marked line. Trim the excess corner fabric ¼" from the stitched line and press.

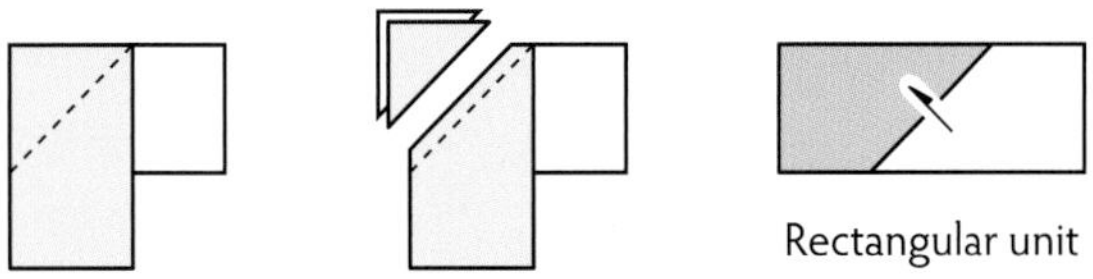

Rectangular unit

To make an elongated flying-geese unit, sew a second rectangle to the opposite end of the base rectangle.

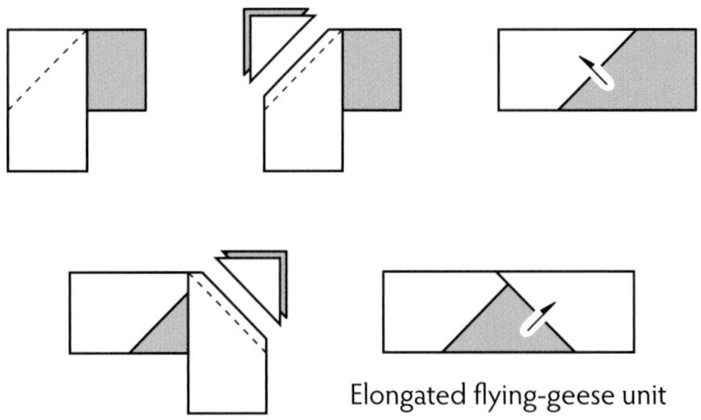

Elongated flying-geese unit

BONUS TRIANGLES

While piecing my blocks, I took the time to stitch a second line on my stitch-and-flip units so that when I trimmed off the corners I was actually trimming off an already pieced half-square-triangle unit (see page 77). You can use these units for any sort of scrap project, but they will be just what you need to make the Baking Day table runner (page 71). Half the work will already be done; you'll just need to press and trim the units to size!

STITCH-AND-FLIP SUCCESS

Practice first. Before working on any new techniques, take the time to practice with scraps.

Find a rhythm that works for you. Some people like to draw the diagonal lines first and then pin them in place. Others like to place the pieces right sides together first, and then draw the line to make sure the angle is correct. Still others (like me) skip marking the lines altogether. See "Ditch the Pencil" on page 78.

Mark your lines carefully. Use a water-soluble marking pen or a temporary fabric-marking pencil to draw your diagonal lines. Because you're sewing on the marked lines, you need to use a marker that won't show through to the front of your quilt and that will be easy to permanently erase if it does bleed through. I do not recommend using heat-soluble fabric markers, as these marks can reappear under certain circumstances.

Piece bonus half-square triangle trimmings. As you're piecing the units, sew a second stitched line toward the corner that you will trim off, ½" from the original stitched line. That way, when you trim off the corners, you're trimming off a half-square-triangle unit that has already been pieced. Just press, trim to the size needed, and the unit is ready to be used in another project.

Try glue basting. If you're having trouble with your pieces wiggling around or shifting as you sew them together (and you don't have plans for your triangle trimmings), try glue basting! Using a water-soluble glue stick, place a tiny dab of glue anywhere on the corner that you'll later trim off and discard. This will help your units stay securely in position when you place them right sides together.

Triangle Units

Throughout this book some units, like large square-in-a-square units and hourglass units, are assembled using triangles. The units are pieced larger than needed, and then trimmed to size for superb precision.

Square It Up

For super-square hourglass units, place a square ruler on top of a unit, aligning the 45° line of the ruler with the diagonal seamline of the unit. Align the midpoint marks on the ruler with the center of the unit. To determine the midpoint marks, divide the size of the unfinished block by two. Trim along the right and top edges of the ruler.

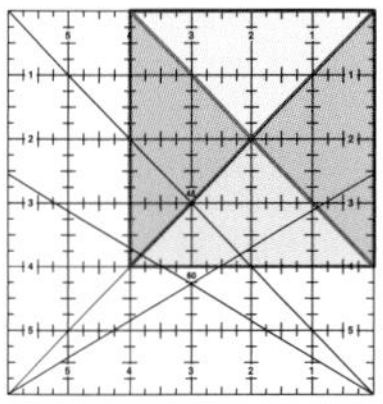

Rotate the unit so that the newly trimmed sides align with the lines of the ruler for the unfinished size of the unit and the 45° line of the ruler is aligned with the diagonal seamline. Trim along the right and top edges of the ruler.

Half-Square-Triangle Units

The half-square-triangle unit is one triangle unit that doesn't actually need to be constructed from triangles. Instead, I eliminate those bias edges by making two units at a time from two squares.

Draw a diagonal line from corner to corner on the wrong side of the lighter square. Pin the marked square on top of a same-sized square, right sides together. Sew ¼" from both sides of the drawn line. Cut the unit apart on the marked line to make two half-square-triangle units. Press the seam allowances in the direction indicated by the arrows. Trim the unit to the size indicated in the pattern.

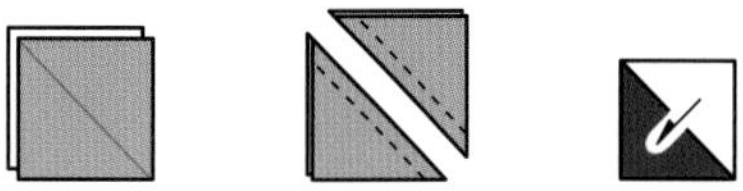

Half-square-triangle unit

Ditch the Pencil

Ready to get rid of your marking tool and try sewing your diagonal seams without marking them first? Just use one of these methods to make a sewing guide line that extends from your needle out along the bed of your sewing machine!

Painter's tape. The simplest way to make a sewing guide line is to place a piece of painter's tape or washi tape on your machine bed. These types of tape won't leave a sticky residue behind. There is even specialized washi tape on the market that has both a sewing line and a ¼" seamline marked on each side for super simple stitching.

Position the tape so that the edge (or stitching line) lines up with the needle of your machine. When you start sewing, line up the first corner with the needle. As you sew, keep the opposite corner lined up with the edge of the tape to stitch a straight line.

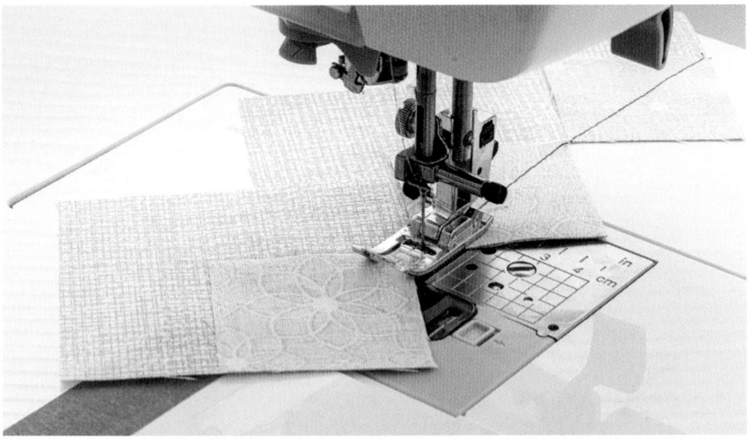

Machine aids. Some machines, like my Bernina 770QE, already have a sewing line marked on the machine bed or extension table. Other machines have laser lights that project the sewing line across the top of your fabric. I've also seen clever quilters mount simple laser beams on their machines to mark their sewing lines. Search online for "sewing machine laser guide" to learn more (and do don't anything that would void your machine's warranty).

Plastic guides. If your machine doesn't have a built-in guide and you don't want to mess with lasers or tapes, try a product like Quilt In A Day's Sew Straight guide. It's a clear plastic guide with a marked stitching line along with some additional diagonal guidelines that temporarily sticks directly to the bed of your machine or extension table.

CONNECT WITH SHELLEY

One of my favorite things about being a quilter is our quilting community! I hope you'll stay in touch and share photos of your own Barn Star projects with us! Here are a few ways we can connect:

Follow me on Instagram @CorasQuilts.

-

Share your own photos on Instagram using #BarnStarSampler and #CorasQuilts so that I can find your projects. Then, follow these hashtags to see more projects from quilty friends!

-

Subscribe to the monthly email newsletter at www.CorasQuilts.com/subscribe. You'll receive links to upcoming blog posts and quilt-alongs—including the Barn Star Quilt-Along coming in 2023—upcoming lectures and workshops, free patterns, and loads of other goodies!

-

Be sure to visit www.CorasQuilts.com/Barn-Stars for more information on how to join our quilt-along community!

ACKNOWLEDGMENTS

The only thing harder than writing your first book is writing your second one! A huge thank you goes out to my quilty family. Words can't express my gratitude.

To my guys—Rob, Aiden, and Jamie. Thanks for your patient and loving support. Thank you for all the frequent stops by my office with hugs and words of encouragement, for ooohing and ahhhing over my latest block, and for keeping me well supplied with snacks and Diet Coke. I couldn't have done this without you. I love you beyond words.

To Cara Cansler of Sew Colorado Quilting for her impeccable and speedy long-arm quilting services and her amazing ability to pick out the perfect quilt design!

To my fabric family at Benartex, not only for providing the materials for this book, but also for helping me curate the perfect fabric collections to bring these quilts to life!

To my friendly book team—thank you for helping me get this project off the ground so quickly and being there to help every step of the way! I can't wait to start our next project together!

ABOUT THE AUTHOR

Photo by Leann Thompson, Leann Marie Photography

Shelley Cavanna is a self-taught quilter, teacher, quilt and textile designer, author, and the owner of Cora's Quilts pattern company. She makes her home near Sacramento, California, with her husband and their two boys. She has a passion for modern, intricate, mosaic-inspired quilts. She makes it her mission to turn these exquisite designs into approachable patterns for quilters of all styles and skill levels, living up to her mantra, "Stunning quilts made simple."

When she's not in the studio, Shelley loves hiking, exploring the nearby Sierra Nevada mountains, and practicing yoga in spite of being a little uncoordinated. She is an avid reader (especially of mysteries and historical fiction), a fan of true-crime podcasts, and a knitter of squishy, cabley sweaters.

Find out more about Shelley's patterns, classes, and quilting adventures at www.CorasQuilts.com.